ADDICTIONS

HYPNOSIS

A Toolkit for Improved Outcomes

Michael S. McGee

LPC, DCH, MS

For those who dare to change and the professionals who help them. Special thanks to all those clients whose courage to change and/or resistance to change made this work possible.

Contents

In the beginning, we were all sober. The beginning of our lives we were active, interested, and curious. A little baby has no use for alcohol, drugs, gambling, or sex. We may crave attention, clean diapers, food, love, and warmth, but we certainly do not look for mom to give us a beer or a joint. Our first "addiction" would most likely be breast milk or formula. That is what one would consider a healthy craving as we need it to survive. As we get a little older, the messages we receive from our culture are to get quick fixes for our ailments. Let's face it, if we have experienced any media or predominant cultural influence, the message appears to be that some drug can fix what ails us.

I presented information titled "Relapse Culture" on this a few years back at a conference where it was very well received. One of the dominant societal communications we are exposed to in this culture is drug use, whether alcohol, prescribed medication, or some other illicit substance. It is certainly hard to maintain sobriety in the face of these messages.

Most persons don't grow up with the ambition to become addicted. We may want to be artists, athletes, craftsmen, entrepreneurs, or scholars. It is pretty obvious that people who become addicted to substances were not trying out for the "team" they end up joining.

For years I have worked with clients who are substance abusers or substance dependent. I have been a student of addictions research since before graduate school. My thesis studies concerned spiritual well being and substance use among college students. Since that time I have worked with varied populations in community service, university campus, and private practice settings. I have used traditional and non-traditional methods with these populations. I believe that traditional treatment methods have their place but are mostly unsuccessful as they often rely heavily on external motivations and penalties for change. The AA approach has been very helpful. It comes from a spiritual model that has been a benefit to many. However, it also falls somewhat into the external motivation category. Most persons do not respond with long lasting change to external motivators. They need a reason within to change.

Research supports the idea that persons change on their own. You might have heard the old song lyrics, "Sick and tired of waking up sick and tired". I find that most persons will "outgrow" their use of substances as they grow and evolve with life. This is more difficult for those who start in early adolescence. They do not seem to learn the appropriate skills and responses needed to cope with the normal ups and downs of life. This may be a result of using substances early on to deal with difficulties and/or as a major means of having fun. If this has happened, they may be "stuck" in adolescent development. These persons will have a lot of growing up to do if they get sober. This can make it even more difficult for them to maintain sobriety. But, for most of us, we would tend to out grow the problem as long as we have not yet reached full blown dependence.

Does this mean we should just wait for change to happen? The answer is, "Of course not". There are ways to find the motivation we need to change and the combination of techniques I will be presenting here are the best methods I know to make this change happen now. Most of the techniques I will be discussing were not developed by me. I just had the vision to combine them in a certain way so that the outcomes are improved. This is powerful stuff. The methods I will talk about are supported by research. However, they have not to my knowledge been used in concert until now. I began to combine them in 2005 and for the last few years my success rate with this population has rapidly improved.

As I have stated, there often comes a time when a person can decide that life as it is no longer works. Some will make an immediate change. Some will even embrace change as refreshing or stimulating. However, this is often a time of ambivalence as many of us are hesitant when faced with change. Some will sit "on the fence", in between, interrupted, or paused in life. This book is about helping people change. The focus is to improve outcomes for those who want change as well as those who are ambivalent. It is about freedom. I mean freedom from addiction specifically and freedom to choose generally. It is about enhancing hypnotic techniques with powerful interviewing methods. It is a path towards a new life. It is about transformation.

When I entered graduate school, motivational interviewing was in its creative beginnings. Miller & Rollnick's (1991) book had just recently been published and "old school" substance abuse counselors seemed to view the method with suspicion as it did not use confrontational techniques that were a mainstay of the more traditional approach in substance abuse treatment. Motivational interviewing is now taught in over 38 languages by hundreds of trainers (Rosengren, 2009). Back then, I was excited. The method struck a chord with me and I embraced the techniques completely. I attended several trainings with MI "experts" and devoured any research produced with the techniques. I also understood immediately that MI could be used for a variety of issues beyond the substance abuse field. It was clear to me that the process of eliciting intrinsic motivation to change could make success more easily obtainable in many clients and/or situations. I felt it was like discovering the Rosetta Stone of therapy. It showed us the language and communication that leads to successful outcomes. MI is useful across multiple intelligence levels and styles of learning. It is a key to consciously unlock our clients from whatever constraints stand in their way. Wherever the client may be on their path to change, MI can assist them to continue the process. And, when it is combined with hypnosis, the combination of conscious and unconscious intrinsic motivation cannot fail to elicit change.

In this book, I wish to provide a framework in which Motivational Interviewing (MI) or Motivational Enhancement Therapy (MET) can be combined with hypnotherapy techniques to create powerful client change. The hypothesis being that as these two therapies are combined, we can assist our clients with maximum therapeutic effect. I will reference research that supports both methods as being statistically effective. I will then describe the techniques in detail that have led to my clinical success in combining these techniques.

My first ten years of being a therapist where spent on the campus of a small liberal arts university working with student substance abusers. I was the only person who met with the students for a time. I can remember teaching and meeting with 177 students in one semester. I would teach a six hour alcohol and drug education course. Then, the students would meet with me individually for a 30 – 50 minute session. It was a high pressure situation. This session was my one chance to make a difference in their lives. I can assure you that no one who entered my program wanted to be there and most had no intention of changing. I developed a style of counseling and education for these students based on MI. At first, it was difficult to keep myself from wanting to direct their actions in healthy ways. Most persons in the helping professions are exposed to this in themselves. We see what they need to do so why don't we just tell them to do it. Think about it. If this worked, we would all obey everything our parents told us to do. Mom and Dad knew what we should do and we always obeyed them. Isn't that right? I know I did everything my parents, teachers, and superiors told me to do. I obeyed them completely, just like my car can fly. Of course, many of our clients know exactly what to do based on the values of others and aren't doing it. So, the puzzle was how to elicit change from within the client.

I was introduced to Miller & Rollnick's (1991) first work on MI about this time. I was excited. This made sense. Get the clients to tell you why they should change and what they should change. Find out what motivates them and utilize it. Do not confront or direct the clients, simply guide them to find their own path towards change. I noticed an immediate change in myself and my clients as I began to utilize these techniques. They actually enjoyed my educational courses. My substance abuse student class evaluations improved so that the angry or disinterested students who entered the class reported leaving with new perspectives and insights. The actual evaluations went from 40 – 50 % positive to 94% positive. This happened because I began to meet the students where they were at on the stages of change. Where was that? Mostly, they were no where. Most of them were not even thinking about change prior to the class unless it was how not to get caught again. I began at that point. Then, I left no one behind. As their expectations and evaluations changed in the classroom, the individual sessions became even more productive. There became no need for confrontation. Resistance became a signal to do things differently or approach the client in another way. The sessions became a sort of dance. The client mostly led and my work got easier. Students who received second alcohol charges were less than 20%. I compared that to recidivism rates in other substance abuse programs and found that some were as high as 80%. I was hooked on MI. This stuff really worked and worked well.

Now, I need to give a little background on myself before explaining how hypnosis techniques begin to play into this scenario. I was a substance abuser for about 20 years. I began early. I was never a cigarette smoker. I can thank my maternal grandfather for that. I got caught smoking cigarettes that we young boys in my social group used to steal at local stores. We were 11 or 12 and could not buy them so we lifted the 25 cent packs and hid out to smoke not thinking that the smell would stay with us. I got caught and my Grandfather had me smoke a pipe loaded full with flavored tobacco. Then, I had to refill it and smoke it down again. Needless to say, I got nicotine poisoning and was deathly sick for hours. That was a quick fix. I still get sick if I smell tobacco smoke. You could say it classically conditioned me to not smoke tobacco. With alcohol I was not so lucky.

My first drink was a hot beer in a tree house at age 11 and it felt good. You could say that right then I was conditioned to enjoy alcohol. You see, the problem with alcohol is you feel good before you get sick or you feel good and never get sick. So, there is always a reward involved for most people. However, I did read that Tony Robbins experienced a way to ensure that one gets the negative effects from alcohol from his Mother who had him "drink like a man" when he first tried beer. He drank beer without stopping until he threw up and that had much the same result as my smoking till I threw up. Though not all persons like the feeling from alcohol, most of the time you can see that liking alcohol can be acquired rather quickly and easily for many. I was no exception and had a family history of alcohol dependence, too. My grandfather had basically drank into death at an early age. There was a lot of alcoholism in the family tree but my Father never touched it. Mostly, this was because he had lost his Father to alcohol. I however, did not have my Father's good sense. So, I started drinking alcohol and kept steadily increasing my quantity and frequency of use over 20 years. At the same time, I began to abuse other substances until I was pretty much diagnosable as poly-substance dependent by age 34. The whole time I worked, went to the gym, and somehow continued to be functional. My wife and children brought me back to reality or down to Earth. And, indeed, I had stayed so high for so long, it was probably a lot like the feeling of being on a crashing plane as it plummeted back to terra firma. Suddenly, I was forced to look at my self, my choices, and my behavior. It was time to change. I had found my self-motivation. It was slow and I had no help but that internal motivation was all I needed to begin the change process.

Unfortunately, I did not seek out a counselor. I am a believer in my own abilities so I rejected AA and NA as they indicated it was beyond my control. I do not recommend that others follow in my foot steps because AA and NA have helped many people. They are good programs. I went "cold turkey". I can honestly say that I have experienced detoxification with no assistance. I do NOT recommend anyone do that either. It was a very bad few days. So, I was sober, alone, and had no idea what to do with myself as my number one coping skill was to drink for most of 20 years. Therefore, I had to mature and develop the coping skills of an adult without help by trial and error. It was not much fun but came to be very rewarding. I sought out self help books. I devoured self help materials by the hundreds both on tape (no CD's back then) and in print. And, I learned about self hypnosis tapes. I was really having difficult times with cravings. I made my first 30 days by toughing it out. I was concerned I would not make it. So, I purchased a "stop drinking" self hypnosis tape and listened to it diligently every day after work when I normally would have attended "happy hour" at the bar. It was incredible. I stopped having any cravings for alcohol or any other substance almost immediately. I became focused on my new life. I envisioned change. Through hypnosis, I could really imagine a wonderful life without using any substances. The changes "took". And, they have lasted over seventeen years. From then on I was determined to go back to school, obtain a formal education in counseling, and learn hypnosis so I could help others to change. This took about 5 more years and was truly worth the effort.

As I mentioned before, during my graduate school training, I was exposed to MI techniques. This was another major turning point. I found a system that would work for most everyone. I knew intuitively that combining MI with hypnosis could be the most powerful tool for change in therapy that anyone could experience. This book is the first piece in the work that shall encompass the entirety of a system for combining MI and hypnosis for successful change.

Motivation

What is motivation? Where does it come from? How do we obtain it? These are some of the questions that we might ask ourselves. How many clients, feeling hopelessly "stuck" in some form of maladaptive or uncomfortable behavior patterns must wonder, "Why can't I get the energy, strength, willpower, or desire to make change happen now and make it last?" The key is motivation.

An accepted psychological model of motivation and how one becomes motivated to action begins with a need. A need is something a person requires for removal of an objective or subjective insufficiency. The awareness of this need will result in the person experiencing a drive. A drive then is an impulse or conscious motivational condition (e.g., hunger, thirst) that leads to creation of a response. A response in turn will be behavior(s) or a sequence of actions with the intention of obtaining a goal. The goal is the intended result of motivated behavior. However, often a goal may also have an incentive value. This means that the goal's attraction to a person is stronger than simply its capacity to fulfill a need. In many instances, this is more significant for successful change to transpire in a rapid and lasting way.

There seem to be three general types of innate or inborn motives for us as humans. There are primary motives. These motives are inborn. Their foundation is in our biological needs and we must meet them in order to survive. For instance, we must eat and drink. Next, there are stimulus motives. Again, these motives appear to be innate and activate us to seek stimulation and information. These needs are key for our growth and learning. Finally, there are secondary motives. These motives result from experience and they are learned needs, drives, and goals. These motives that we learn can be related to our culture and social interaction. They would be acquired by growing up in a particular society or culture and as such are often called social motives. Persons might also be motivated by a need for achievement or desire to meet some subjective standard of excellence. And, often people may find that a need for power becomes a strong motivator in their lives as they want to have influence or command over others.

Abraham Maslow, often referred to as the "Father of Motivational Psychology", took the idea of needs much farther. His is well known for developing a Hierarchy of Human Needs. Maslow's classification of needs is based on their supposed power or potency among us. Therefore, some needs are more potent than others. Those more powerful needs will influence our thoughts and actions to a greater degree. The first four levels of needs in Maslow's hierarchy are referred to as the Basic Needs. These lower needs tend to be more potent than higher needs as they must be met for basic survival and social interaction to occur. These have also been referred to as deficiency needs vs. growth needs. These lower needs are called deficiency needs as when one experiences their lack it is clear for there will be uncomfortable physical and/or psychological reactions until the needs are sufficiently met. Maslow believed that lower needs in the hierarchy are dominant. Once these lower needs are achieved, we are free to explore Growth or Meta-Needs. These needs were considered to be of a higher level by Maslow. These higher-level needs associated with impulses for self-actualization and self-actualization itself. Basic needs must be satisfied before growth motives are fully expressed. Desires for self-actualization are reflected in various meta-needs. In moving towards self actualization, persons become more able to clearly see human nature in all its good and evil with acceptance and non-judgment. These people accept the challenges of life as they come along and actively seek solutions. They are more concerned with the good of all humans than themselves. They seem to understand the need for solitude and contemplation in finding resolutions to difficulties. They have a positive sense of humor, high ethical standards, and quest for knowledge. In order for change to occur, these motives must be active and examples of self actualization are often expresses by those persons who reach the stage of transcending limiting behaviors such as addictions.

Where does motivation come from? Basically, science tells us that there can only be two sources. Most theorists believe it comes from within or without the person. These two sources are known as intrinsic and extrinsic motivations. Intrinsic Motivation comes from within the person (internal), not from external results or rewards and is often based on personal pleasure of being involved in an action or task. Extrinsic Motivation is considered to result from obvious external rewards, obligations, or similar factors (e.g., pay, grades).

My personal opinion is that this is erroneous. True motivation only comes from within. The incentive may be external but the motivation to act must be internal for anything to actually change. In reactance theory, Brehm (1966) proposes that when persons feel that their freedom to choose is being limited or personal freedoms are threatened, the result will be an aversion to change. Imagine someone who thinks they know best for you telling you what to do. How many times has this happened to us and how did it feel? What goes wrong? We need a reason to change based on our individual goals and/or values, not based on the advice, criticisms, manipulations, coercions, rewards, or demands of others. Brehm believed that external pressures to change could actually result in less desire to change. The person will become paradoxically more opposed to changing. There is social psychological research which supports this hypothesis and even indicates that external rewards for behaviors that are intrinsically motivated may have a harmful effect (Tang & Hall, 1995). That is, when rewarded for doing something we already enjoy (intrinsically), we tend to decrease our attraction or enjoyment of the activity. This is known as the over justification effect. This phenomenon occurs when incentives are used to bring about actions that would have been done voluntarily without any external reinforcement. Based on this information, I believe that the only valuable motivation for successful change is from within.

Ambivalence

When it comes to change, many of us react with hesitation and ambivalence. Ambivalence derives from the Latin prefix *ambi*, meaning "both" and *valentia*, meaning "strength". It is common to use the word "ambivalent" to describe a lack of feelings one way or the other towards issues or circumstances. However, this seems odd as it would seem that strong feeling/thoughts for more than one choice are implied. A more standard word to use in the instance of lack of feeling, however, would be "indifferent". Proper usage is to remember that the prefix *ambi* means "both", so if you are "ambivalent", you have both strong positive and negative feelings towards something, or have strong feelings for both sides of an issue. Ambivalence is defined as the experience of having simultaneous, conflicting thoughts or feelings toward a person, thing, or choice. Ambivalence can be the state of having thoughts and emotions of both positive and negative aspects toward someone or something. Often, people have mixed feelings about change. Staying the same frequently provides stability and consistency that reduces anxiety. Change might be considered a threat. Commonly, people use an example of the feeling of both attraction and repulsion or "love-hate" for a person to describe ambivalence. The term also refers to situations where "mixed feelings" are experienced, or where a person experiences uncertainty or indecisiveness concerning something. The expressions of "cold feet" and "sitting on the fence" are phrases often used to express ambivalence. Or, for our usage, I recommend that we describe it as having strong feelings for more than one option that inhibit choice.

Ambivalence can be psychologically disagreeable when the good and not so good features of a subject are both present in a person's thoughts simultaneously. This can lead to avoidance or procrastination reactions. A person might also make calculated efforts to make their mind up concerning the ambivalence. When the conditions do not involve the need for a decision, people encounter less distress even when feeling ambivalent. I have noted that the standard approach to ambivalence indicates the choice involves strong positive and negative aspects. Most persons use this narrow definition. However, in psychologically defining conflicts of this nature, choices often come in three basic types. The first, as noted in most ambivalence research, is an approach/avoidance conflict. This signifies that there are both positive and negative aspects to a decision. Second is an approach/approach conflict. Here, ambivalence can also occur as either choice can be pleasant and the decision can be even more difficult. Finally, there is the possibility of an avoidance/avoidance conflict in which both choices seem to have negative aspects. In any of the three conflicts, a person might experience ambivalence. So, we cannot focus only on positive/negative but in each case a decisional balance must be explored as to the choice which seems the best at the time in order to "get off the fence" and move towards change.

We must assume ambivalence is present or else the client would have completed the change with no therapeutic assistance. We must not assume the client is "resistant" when it is often normal to be ambivalent about change. When a person is resistant to change it is very likely that they have unresolved ambivalence. It would be more correct to label this phenomenon as such. Change is stressful. When I write about avoidance/avoidance conflict I am sure that both choices will lead to stress. The goal for getting off of the fence then would be to seek the one that may be least stressful. Even an approach/approach conflict can lead to stress. For instance, if I am working on losing weight and I have a choice between a Caesar salad with grilled chicken (healthy) and a rich pasta meal (not so healthy) when I love the taste/enjoy eating both. I will be attracted to both and most likely be ambivalent as I weigh my choice. Either way, my stomach will be happy with the choice but I may think that eating the salad will mean my hunger will return more quickly or eating the pasta may make it more difficult to lose weight. So, even when both choices will make me feel good, one must create less distress for me to decide. Better yet, what about marriage? I want to marry (good) and I enjoy being single (good). Am I ambivalent? The answer may well be, "yes". Often, many people can be "on the fence" about this decision. The stress can be very high and both outcomes may feel good. The idea here is that any and all decisions might occur after the resolution of ambivalence. No matter what the value of the possible choices. "Resistance" may indeed just be the natural consequence of ambivalence to change and therefore useless for us to consider as such.

Anxiety or fear is not an abnormal condition when considering a major change. Staying the same is stable and safe. Change indicates a confrontation with the unknown or unfamiliar. It is uncharted territory. Many persons are reluctant to enter these "new worlds". Many persons would much rather leave the exploring to someone else. One key to helping resolve ambivalence would be alleviating anxiety concerning change. The hypnotherapist has the advantage here as relaxation is an integral component of the hypnotic process. Hypnotic relaxation is frequently a part of therapy for anxious or fearful clients. In theory, the relaxed client will be more inclined to embrace change and less likely to be ambivalent. Therefore, I strongly suggest a relaxation exercise in session for the very first visit in order to assist this process. I also like to suggest a simple acronym that may be helpful to clients and counselors alike at this stage:

- **AGA ©**
- **Accept** – you cannot solve a problem by attacking it (war language). Focus on increasing the positive instead. Taking offense weakens us
- **Gratitude** – seek things to be grateful for
- **Allow** – open to connecting with your creative intentions

(AGA © copyright protected)

Motivational Interviewing

Our primary method for overcoming ambivalence is increasing intrinsic motivation through client interviewing techniques. Motivational Interviewing (MI) was first introduced in 1983 by Miller. Together in 1991, Miller and Rollnick collaborated to structure the techniques we know today as MI. The method was initially formed as a combination of relationship-building principles from Carl Rogers' (1951) Humanistic Theory with certain Cognitive-Behavioral therapy strategies (Burke, Arkowitz, & Menchola, 2003). Also, Miller and Rollnick developed the techniques in such a way as to engage the client at their particular point of motivation based on the Stages of Change model (Prochaska & DiClemente, 1984). Motivational interviewing is non-judgmental, non-confrontational and non-adversarial. The method assists to intensify the client's awareness of the probable difficulties caused, consequences, and risks involved as outcomes of the behavior in question. Alternatively, therapists help clients imagine a better future, and become progressively more motivated to achieve it. This is very beneficial in conquering our natural tendency to be ambivalent. Regardless, the strategy assists clients to think in new ways about their actions and eventually contemplate what might be achieved through change.

Motivational Interviewing is intentionally more directive than Rogers yet maintains a client-centered approach to counseling that is more focused and goal-directed than nondirective counseling. The original intention was to assist clients that might be struggling with issues about or ambivalence to change. It was created with four basic principles in mind; expressing empathy, developing discrepancy, rolling with resistance, and supporting the client's self-efficacy. These principles are designed to "help free people from the ambivalence that entraps them in repetitive cycles of self-defeating or self-destructive behaviors" (Miller & Rollnick, 2002). This concept can be easily expanded to include any thoughts or behaviors that a client may wish to change. MI is not so much just a counseling technique, but to a certain extent instead it is an interpersonal style of communication that is not just restricted to formal settings. This idea of interpersonal style is essential to successful MI and the manner in which it is to be employed.

The research on successful change through motivational interviewing is pretty significant. Burke, Arkowitz, and Menchola (2003) found that MI was significantly related to positive change in studies of alcohol, diet, drug use, exercise, smoking, and weight loss. When I discovered this and compared it to results from hypnosis research it was easy to theorize on the way that these two techniques could be combined holistically in order to create a more powerful method for treatment. Much of this effect may also be related to the assistance of MI towards enhancing rapport between client and therapist. Again, research on therapeutic rapport and treatment outcomes seems to support the use of these methods as rapport and empathy are powerful tools for effective communication and change. (Eagan, 1982; Miller, 1980; Truax & Carkhuff, 1967; Truax & Mitchell, 1971; Valle, 1981).

MI contains several key components. First and most importantly, the motivation to change comes from within the client (intrinsic motivation). It is based on their values, intentions, and goals. Secondly, it is the client's responsibility to resolve his or her ambivalence. The therapist's primary function is to guide the client. This is effectively accomplished by reflective listening (Burke, Arkowitz, & Menchola, 2003). The counselor is somewhat directive, but only in assisting the client to discover the source of his or her ambivalence. This guidance towards discovery is an art that often leads to resolution. The counselor must avoid direct persuasion and/or confrontation. In fact, it is best if the presentation maintains a calm style that assists clients to bring forth their own answers. One might believe that direct persuasion is helpful but it often results in client resistance and gets in the way of progress towards change. One moves through the stages of change when readiness is achieved. The readiness to change depends upon intrinsic motivation and the quality of the interpersonal relationships among clients and therapists. Therefore, the final element of MI is the interaction between the client and therapist. This relationship is intended to be more like a partnership or companionship rather than an expert/recipient role (Miller & Rollnick, 2002).

Motivational Interviewing is designed with the intention of assisting people to navigate the change process. It always begins with meeting the client where they are in the change process. This is much like the hypnotic techniques of Milton Erickson which will be discussed later on. The Stages of Change are a part of the Trans-theoretical Model of Change. This model attempts to describe how people change and is not a theory of psychopathology (MIA: STEP, 2006). This model assists therapists from various theoretical systems in finding common ground from where to examine and assist the change process. The stages of change are as follows: pre-contemplation, contemplation, preparation, action, and maintenance (MIA: STEP, 2006). Prochaska and DiClemente (1986) include a sixth stage when dealing with addictions and that stage is relapse. I personally do not use the term relapse and will explain why when I describe the stages in more detail. I also like to use the term transcendence for a final stage in which persons have transformed their lives in such a way as to never be able to go back to previous detrimental behaviors.

Let's talk briefly about the stages of change. Pre-contemplation is a state where a person has no thought of changing either now or later. Friends, family, law enforcement or others may repeatedly urge us to take action on our problem and yet we have no intention of changing. The thought of this client is most likely something like, "What do you mean change?" This client has not even considered change. Indeed, they are not considering changing or quitting the behavior in at any time in the next 6 months. Often, when working with persons who have received a first alcohol or drug violation with the legal system, they are at this stage of change.

When a person enters Contemplation, they have began to consider change. However, at this point they are frequently still feeling a lot of ambivalence concerning change. They may still be "on the fence" so to speak. They may be wondering about their habits or behaviors. It may be wondering about how change would be or wondering about why they have stayed the same so long. They might certainly need assistance in evaluating the pros and cons of their actions and of the change they are considering. We might consider the payoffs for not changing and compare them with the payoff for change. This is a time for self exploration and finding understanding. They might ask themselves, "Hummm, I wonder if I should change and how that might be for me?" The rational mind and the emotions must be brought into balance with a focus on commitment to change. Persons at this stage begin to seriously consider the implications of change, quitting something that does not serve their best interest, or taking action in ways that bring benefits to themselves. They may be on the fence but they are seriously considering jumping off within the next 6 months.

When a person decides to change, then they move into Preparation. This is the planning stage. All goals require a plan to be successful. At this point, it is key to develop a plan of action or intention. What is intention? It is a plan of action or an aim that guides an action. The Latin root *intentio* means to stretch toward. This indicates a bit of discomfort along with growth. In medical terminology, it is the course or manner of healing a wound. Remember that healed tissue is always stronger than the original. This also indicates strength and improvement. Intention precedes action and requires aligning one's conscious desires in such a way as to guarantee success. It is recommended that all clients write down a change plan to be discussed and utilized for the hypnotic session. This is a conscious act of making intention concrete. "Ok, I need to make a plan here. What will I do?" It is often helpful to identify temptations, remove them, and find ways to avoid them. The clients may need to arrange for interpersonal support systems. They may need to plan for substitute behaviors that assist to effectively replace old behaviors or patterns in such a way as they are not missed. Clients in preparation are planning to eliminate or change behaviors soon often in the next 30 days or less.

Eventually, persons will begin to actually behave, think, and/or feel different. This is the Action stage of change. In this stage, they are actually doing the work. The persons begin to take needed actions and steps that move them towards change. They will most likely have created a change plan during preparation, but, producing the plan may be a form of action, too. Often, change will not occur without a person taking the time to actually plan for success. In a plan, they can describe concrete reasons for change, focus on actual steps to be taken, brainstorm ways that others might help them, and plan for obstacles. As they actively implement their plans, they begin to actually practice their new behaviors. Action stage occurs during the first 6 months of changed behavior.

Once the new behavior has been actively consistent for over 6 months, a person is considered to be in Maintenance stage. As the person continues to "do" and act in new way (s), they are at the point of simply maintaining their change. They are in process of learning how it feels to act/be different. They have been doing things differently for a while now and are in a period of adjustment. Often, they are adjusting to the changes as are significant others around them. They are dealing with any concerns, new stresses, or difficulties that might arise. They might be involved in learning or utilizing new strengths and coping skills. This can be uncomfortable at first for some persons but each success adds to the new positive picture of life. A person can develop a new sense of pride and self esteem from their new successes.

Eventually, the process of maintenance will no longer be "new". Not only has a new behavior been in use for some time but it is the "normal" way for the person to behave. When this happens, transcendence has occurred. A client is now free to be a "new" person. Not only is the behavior no longer a part of their life but they would never consider going back to their old habits or behaviors. It would seem to be abnormal now. They have re-invented themselves. Much like the caterpillar emerges completely changed into the butterfly, the client cannot go back. At any point in the process a person may go back to previous actions prior to transcendence but not afterward.

However, prior to transcendence, a person may return to any previous stage. They can go all the way back to pre-contemplation though this would be more difficult as the memory of passing through more advanced stages interferes with the ability to be the "same old person". This is not a relapse. I detest that term. It is merely a lapse, a trip, or stumble on the path. It is not failure. It is a return to the safety of the familiar and quite likely a normal component of the change process. It may be very helpful to the process to return to old behavior patterns and find they no longer work. This can result in more rapid and powerful change. It is important to support this process without condemning or judging the client. Frequently, they may be their harshest critic and the therapist's non-judgmental support can act as a bridge to return to the spiral of change.

So you might see how it is very important to "Do the right thing at the right time" for hypnosis to be most effective. When seeking to enhance a client's intrinsic motivation to change, it is imperative that we identify activities that modify thinking, feeling, and behaving based on the client's current stage of change. The therapist will employ diverse approaches and procedures in effort to meet the clients' needs based on the clients' current stage of change. This model (Stages of Change) is based on a progression through the different stages, but not everyone reaches the desired change at the same rate and not everyone continues "forward". Some individuals may cycle back to an earlier stage as part of their process, others may move forward through each stage and never look back, while some may recycle through the various stages several times before achieving their goals and maintaining change over time.

We must gently assist the client with careful reflections and targeted questioning to access the next level. To conduct an effective client interview requires that we approach in an empathetic, insightful, affirming, and motivating way. Then, hypnotic interventions may be utilized that have the correct focus for the client's current and future stage. Research indicates that this is of primary importance. The beginning approaches are outlined in detail by Prochaska, Norcross, and DiClemente (1994) in their book titled, "Changing For Good: A Revolutionary Six-Stage Program for Overcoming Bad Habits and Moving Your Life Positively Forward". The initial investigation of the stages of change was completed with a population of cigarette smokers and the results were impressive (DiClemente, 1983; Prochaska, & DiClemente, 1983; Prochaska, DiClemente, & Norcross, 1992; Prochaska, et al., 1994). These studies show that using the stages of change model will improve smoking cessation outcomes. If we look at the research concerning hypnosis for smoking cessation we find similar positive outcomes. It is suggested in many studies that most persons who experienced hypnosis for smoking cessation have success (Lynn, Neufeld, Rhue, & Matorin, A., 1993). Also, Crasilneck (1990) reported that at 12 month follow up 81% of clients who were hypnotized to stop smoking were still abstinent. If using motivation and the stages of change is successful and hypnosis alone is successful in smoking cessation. What will happen when the two are combined? I was determined to explore the possibilities.

The standard "magical myth" of hypnosis is that change occurs immediately in one session and is long lasting, but the model of change does not indicate that this is necessarily true. Particularly, there are amazing success stories in the field of hypnosis but immediate change does not occur in all cases. In an effort to improve outcomes, it may be prudent to follow a model of change in stages and develop a hypnotic treatment protocol that while directive is also client centered based on the stage of change a client may be in at the time of intake and movement towards each successive stage of change.

One of the first things asked by interns training with me was simply, "How do I know what stage a client is in?" It is often not very difficult. For instance, if client's report that they have not had any problem or issues for over 6 months, it is most likely that they have achieved maintenance. If they are currently involved in some type of active behavioral pursuit of change within less than 6 months, they are probably involved in action stage. If they state an intention to begin changes and/or are formulating a plan for change in the next month or so, this is a clear indication of preparation. If their intention to change is not so immediate or if they state they are thinking about changing sometime in the next 6 months, they are most likely in contemplation of change (and often very ambivalent about it). And, if they do not speak of changing at all or report that things are just fine the way they are right now, this is a pretty clear indication of pre-contemplation. You may even consider adding the following statements to your intake questionnaire with yes or no response indicators:

1. I resolved my difficulty more than six months ago.

   Yes ___ No ___

2. I have been actively working on the problem in the past 6 months.

   Yes ___ No ___

3. I plan to do something about this in the next month or so.

   Yes ___ No ___

4. I am thinking or planning to do something about this in the next 6

   months.   Yes ___ No ___

5. I am fine just as I am.   Yes ___ No ___

Please remember, if there are "no" responses to the first four statements or a yes to number 5 the client is most likely in pre-contemplation. Utilizing these simple statements or careful questioning and active listening will most likely result in the information we require to assess what stage a client may be in at the time of our session.

The Therapeutic Basics for Success

Motivational Enhancement Therapy provides a protocol for using MI in order to assist the client in rapidly moving towards change while enhancing intrinsic motivation and was conceptualized originally for specific use in the area of alcohol abuse/dependence and researched during Project MATCH (Project MATCH Research Group, 1997). In a Meta-analysis involving 15 MI Randomized control studies where MI was compared with "usual/brief/standard" care, directive-confrontational counseling, educational interventions, skills based counseling, and cognitive behavioral therapy alone, it was indicated that MI was most effective for client change.

Miller and Rollnick (2002) used the acronym FRAMES to describe the six elements they believe are active ingredients in producing change in substance abusers. FRAMES stands for feedback of personal risk, emphasizing client's responsibility for change, advice concerning change, eliciting a menu of options, expressing empathy, and developing self-efficacy. These six elements can be utilized in motivational enhancement therapy for a majority of individuals, not just those suffering from substance abuse disorders (Motivational Enhancement Therapy Manual, 1994). The therapist uses structured feedback regarding the behavior, severity of the behavior, and the current stage of the client to elicit self-motivated and rapid change. Therefore, this therapy is adding a sense of urgency and ultimately is "superior for enhancing readiness to change" (Dunn, Neighbors, & Larimar, 2006).

We know that MI and MET are successful and valid techniques for change. The research on hypnosis parallels MI research. The treatments are also for the same client populations, that is, substance abuse, diet, exercise, and weight loss groups (Burke, Arkowitz, & Menchola, 2003; Carels, Darby, Cacciapaglia, Konrad, Coit, & Harper, et al., 2007; Dunn, Neighbors, & Larimer, 2006; Hutchinson-Phillips, & Gow, 2005; Kirsch, Montgomery, & Sapirstein,1995; Nigg, Burbank, Padula, Dufresne, Rossi, & Velicer, et al., 1999; Pederson, Scrimgeour, & Lefcoe, 1975; Prochaska, Velicer, Rossi, Goldstein, Marcus, Rakowski, Fiore, Harlow, Redding, Rosenbloom, & Rossi, 1994; Sarkin, Johnson, Prochaska, & Prochaska, 2001). Pederson, et al. (1975) completed a preliminary study of combining hypnosis with cognitive techniques and found that the efficacy of both were enhanced by their combination. I considered this to be somewhat of a confirmation that I must be on the right track. In order to create the best possible combination for my clients' success, I wanted to put these techniques together. It was very clear to me. If we have powerful and statistically significant change resulting from both MI and hypnosis by themselves, how might our treatment outcomes improve if we "marry" the two techniques? Hence, the motivational hypnosis concept for change began to come together in my mind. Quickly, I integrated these techniques into my practice and started to talk about them with colleagues. After four years of working in practice with the combined techniques, I presented my first ideas at the American Society of Clinical Hypnosis' 50th Anniversary Scientific Meeting & Workshops in Chicago, IL, March 2008. The audio version of this presentation should still be available from the ASCH.

The MI standards that will be most helpful for us as therapists have been written about extensively by Miller & Rollnick (2002). I strongly suggest the reader exam their original works to become intimately familiar with the details of the approach. The main goals of motivational interviewing are to establish rapport, elicit change talk, and establish commitment language from the client. Keep in mind that rapport has been indicated as the primary indicator of successful therapy regardless of method (Burke, Arkowitz, & Menchola, 2003; Egan, 1982; Miller, 1980; Truax & Carkhuff, 1967; Truax & Mitchell, 1971; Valle, 1981). The process we are using is to develop a client centered approach to evoke intrinsic motivation.The four basic principles are to express empathy, develop discrepancies, roll with resistance, and support self efficacy (Miller & Rollnick).

Empathy has many different definitions. They cover a broad range from a feeling of concern for other people that produces an intention to help them, experiencing feelings that correspond with another person's emotions, identifying what the other person is thinking or feeling, to blurring the line between self and other. For our purposes, empathy is the therapist's ability to accurately recognize the client's meaning and reflect the correct understanding back to the client. Empathy is NOT having had the same experience or difficulty. It is not a feeling of identification with the client or telling your own story as in self disclosure. As described by Carl Rogers (1959), empathy leads to correct understanding. Thus, it is sensing the pain or the pleasure of another as he or she perceives it and to notice the causes thereof as he or she perceives them, but without ever losing the awareness that it is as if the therapist were hurt or pleased, etc (Rogers). Rogers (1961) also described how one may combine empathy with warmth and genuineness to enhance the therapeutic relationship. Warmth demonstrates unconditional positive regard, that is, acceptance and encouragement of a person regardless of what the person says or does. It is an attitude that values clients even when aware of their failings. The therapist and client must be honest and genuine in this relationship and empathy assists this process. Genuineness creates trust. Therefore, the therapist is providing the best possible conditions for personal growth to the client. Empathy is active listening with goal of understanding. However, MI adds a goal direction component that was not a part of Rogers' original work.

Developing discrepancy, guides therapists to assist clients in appreciating the value of change by examining the incongruity between how clients currently live their lives to how they would like them to be (or between their core values and their day-to-day actions). Remember that clients are often ambivalent about change. By developing their awareness of ambivalence and these discrepancies in their behaviors, we shift the decisional balance in the direction of change. We simply aid the client in determining how the current behavior is blocking or detrimental to the person's needs, goals, values, or hopes for the future. The behavior may be a major barrier to their dreams for the future. Becoming aware of this often allows the person to make their own arguments for change.

When the client is telling you the reason they must end their addiction, your part in the process becomes monumentally less difficult.

Resistance is a natural part of the change process. Remember, most clients have mixed feelings about change. For many, staying the same provides stability and consistency that reduces anxiety. Change might be considered a threat. Therapists who roll with resistance demonstrate an acceptance of a client's reluctance to change as natural and not pathological. This will enhance rapport and increase the odds of successful change. If the client is resistant it is your problem not theirs. It is a clear indication that the therapist is doing something wrong. It often means that clients feel they are being forced in a particular direction, their thought/feelings are being ignored, or that there is no empathy. Remember, resistance is merely a behavior and is not really personal. To avoid this, we must be careful not to argue for change. The clients must inform us as to why change is preferable. Their view is superior to ours. It is often a symptom of the extreme dissonance or ambivalence they are experiencing. Resistance should not be opposed directly. It takes two to make resistance work. Resistance is highly responsive to the style of the therapist. It is a signal to the therapist. Resistance is your cue to choose a different response or a new direction. You are not directing the changes. You are seeking to aid the clients in choosing their most appropriate path to success. The best approach may be simply to "back off" and let the client explore their own ideas and options for a time. Thus, the relationship will not be damaged and mutual respect is maintained.

Therapists who support self efficacy are embracing client autonomy. They respect the client's right to choose (even when clients choose to not change). This assists clients to move toward change successfully and with confidence, knowing the decision is their own. The person (NOT the counselor) is responsible for choosing and carrying out change. It is helpful to reinforce any small successes along the way. It is important for the clients to be aware of their own abilities and ego strengthening techniques may be utilized to improve this sense of personal power. A person's belief in the possibility of change is an important motivator for this choice to occur. The therapist's belief in change is quite important also. If a therapist believes the client cannot succeed, even on an unconscious level, this message will most likely become a part of the client's awareness. So, it is absolutely necessary that the therapist believe in both the possibility and likelihood of change being successful. The client will become aware of this on one or more levels and it will affect his or her confidence to succeed. However, in the end, it all comes down to the clients. Their choices and their beliefs are the keys to change.

How do we most effectively use motivational interviewing? Miller and Rollnick (2002) wrote of some basic counseling skills involved in the MI process and moving a client from ambivalence into actual movement towards change. The first four are directly from Client Centered Therapy by Rogers (1951). These are use open ended questions, affirm the client's actions toward change and use basic ego strengthening techniques, utilize reflection (sometimes with a twist), and summarize back to the client your understanding of what was shared. Also, a final skill that is required would be the ability to elicit talk of change from the client. These are the foundation for this practice to be effective.

As a trained counselor or therapist, we may all know the difference between open and closed questions, but, a brief review could be helpful for clarification. If I am asking a closed question then it will be limited to a short answer, a yes/no answer, just the basic or specific information, or some type of multiple choice question. These approaches all result with limited response options. They restrict the interview and do not allow for expansion or creativity on the client's part. The following are some examples of closed questions:

- Do you like to smoke?
- When did you start smoking?
- Does your family care about this?
- Do you want to quit, slow down, or just stay the same?

However, an open ended question will "open the door" for expanded narrative answers. Open questions do not encourage short answers but often require thought and allow for the entire story to be shared. Examine the following questions.

- What would you like from treatment?
- Where do you see yourself as far as _____(habit or behavior) in 5 years?
- Tell me about your_____ (habit or behavior)? What are the good things about it? What are the not so good things?
- If you were to quit, how would you do it?

There are some effective guidelines for getting better results from questions. One, it is always advisable to ask fewer questions. More questions often lead to more closed questions and less time for the client to respond fully with their complete story. Two, it is not appropriate to ask multiple questions in a row. If you ask more than three questions in rapid succession, it is highly unlikely that you will get answers to all of them. If you do receive answers to all of them, it is very likely that they will be incomplete or possibly miss information that may prove to be vital to the success of therapy. Third, it is very likely that you will have to ask some closed questions to fill in details and facts during a client interview. But, it is essential that the therapist ask more open than closed questions. Closed questions are to be used very sparingly and only when you feel that pertinent details may be missing from the client's narrative in response to open inquiries. Finally, it may often be helpful to offer double reflections for each question response. This allows an opportunity for one reflection to be much closer to the meaning a client wishes to convey and might show that there is more than one interpretation of events, therefore, opening the possibility for a client to also interpret the situation in multiple ways. Some interpretations can be more helpful than others.

Most hypnotherapists are familiar with ego strengthening and client affirmation techniques. It is important while conducting MI that these techniques are used to promote the ability to change. We must seek opportunities to assist the client's belief in his or her own ability to make change happen. This is done by "catching them at success" and making sure they note it. It is also a function of the language the therapist uses. We want to highlight any client strengths or successes in order to promote the idea of success and client self efficacy. We must be sure that both we and the clients notice and appreciate positive actions both past and present. Then, inquire as to how these actions might be useful in the future for change. As therapists, we must be genuine. There is nothing worse than a client finding a therapist to be less than open or honest in the relationship. Never forget that the client deserves unconditional positive regard and be observant for opportunities to express this in caring, concerned language. These techniques will aid in strengthening the therapeutic relationship and a strong, positive relationship is one key to success.

There are some basic ways to develop ego strength. One might simply comment positively on a client characteristic, such as, "You're a strong person, a survivor". A therapist could make a straightforward statement of appreciation, like, "I appreciate your openness and honesty today". There are many opportunities to catch clients doing something right. One can use simple ego strengthening statements, for instance, "Thanks for coming today" "That's right", or "Very good". Genuine compliments akin to, "I like the way you said that" or "I am impressed by the way you handled that" can be very helpful. Uncomplicated expressions of hope, caring, or support, similar to, "I hope this weekend goes well for you" might be all that is needed to increase the client's intrinsic ability and confidence to do well.

After a client has responded to a question, an appropriate reflection from the therapist will often assist him or her to explore alternatives or look more realistically at current behaviors. Remember that reflections should be made more in the form of statements rather than questions. A reflection states a hypothesis or speculation about what the person means. The therapist is making a guess about the client's meaning. This does not necessarily mean that the therapist is correct though ideally this will be the case. Appropriate reflections will result in more information along with better understanding of the client's subjective reasoning and perceptions of events involved. Often, some questions might be changed to a reflection. In order to form a statement, not a question, think of the question in terms of something like, "Do you mean that you_____?" Then, you may simply remove the first for words and say simply, "You _____."

You will want to modulate your voice so that your volume decreases at end for the statement. This allows for the client to feel that they are able to respond with correction if need be and helps to eliminate the feeling that you are certain of their meaning. This implies that the client is the expert and the therapist is striving for deeper understanding without shutting down any chance to disagree with the reflection. We also need to be brief. We do not wish to monopolize this time with our own thoughts. Work to keep reflections brief and no longer than client's statement.

Reflections may be divided into five uncomplicated styles for our purposes. Remember always that we are demonstrating that we understand the world view of our clients with accuracy along with the emotional components and meanings. We are showing we can interpret reality as if we were the person. Thus, we exhibit our ability to sense the hurt or the pleasure of another as he or she senses it. We appear to perceive the causes of the situation as he or she perceives them. The first, simple reflection has been previously described by one method, the "you" statement. Other ways to use simple reflection might be to repeat and share the client's statement. We can also respond with a metaphor that is a direct reflection and includes imagery. A client may offer, "It seems everyone is against me". A simple metaphoric reflection may be, "It is like you are surrounded by pests that keep biting at you". Another reflection method is agreement with a shift. I will often shift the reflection to elicit change talk. For instance, a client may state, "Smoking is the only way I can relax". To this I might reply, "Up until now, you thought smoking was your only option for relaxation". This response is a reflection that allows for options and change talk. Third, we may use a double sided reflection to emphasize ambivalence. A client might state, "I don't want to quit drinking completely". To which I might respond with, "You can see that there are problems related to your alcohol use, but you are not prepared to think about completely quitting. What would help?" Fourth, we may reframe a client's negative interpretation of events with a positive twist. If the client were to say, "Everyone is always nagging me about my smoking". We could respond with, "It sounds like people are worried about you even though they make you upset. Maybe, we can help them to show their concerns in a way that is helpful to you. What are some ways they can help?" Finally, we may just have to side with the negative. You must use caution with this approach. If your relationship with the client is not secure this can be detrimental to the relationship. The client might offer, "I love to drink. I don't think I can change if I want to." And you could agree, "Drinking is more important to you than anything and you cannot quit". If you use this method, it can result in an explosion of emotion. Be careful. Use only as a last resort.

Once you feel that your questions for the session are exhausted. You need to put it all together for both yourself and the client. In a way, this is similar to making a collection of the material that has been expressed and returning it to the client in an easily understandable form so that the evolving script is no surprise. A good summary for a client who has come to you to quit smoking might sound like, "So far you've expressed concern about keeping your job in a smoke-free facility, improving your health, and removing the odor of smoke from your car, clothes, and home." You may wish to link something more recently expressed with something discussed earlier, "That sounds like what you said about that anxious feeling you get". We want to put it all together and then transition. "Before we move on to the hypnosis session, I need to ask, do you think we have covered everything so far".

There are some questioning "traps" to steer clear of and avoid setting up client resistance (Miller & Rollnick; 1998, 2002). Always, we are keeping in mind that the client is most likely ambivalent about change. Resistance is merely a signal to the therapists that we are doing something wrong. A client who is not in rapport with the therapist is not likely to change, regardless of tactics, whereas, a client who feels empathy and understanding from the therapist is very likely to succeed.

First, we need to be cautious of being ensnared with the "Question-Answer" interaction. In this type of situation, the client merely responds to questions and does not elaborate on any subject. Avoid asking direct closed questions such as: "You're here to quit smoking, right?" "Do you think you smoke too much?" "What is your favorite time to smoke?" As you may guess, these questions do not allow for a narrative to emerge and might actually shut down effective communication. This is a sure sign that things are not going well.

Second, we must beware of taking sides and initiating a confrontation. If a client states, "My wife nags me all the time to quit drinking." A "taking sides" response might be, "Your wife is worried about your use. It appears your drinking is out of control." A more appropriate reflection could be, "It sounds like your wife is worried about you. How might things be better between you?" This is more likely to reveal motivations to change. It will also enhance the rapport, whereas, taking a stance does not allow the client freedom to explore his or her

own options and may create animosity. Empathy and rapport are more important for successful therapy. The client is the expert on his or her life.

Third, do not get caught up in your own expertise. Again, the client is the expert. We do not have all of the answers. In our desire to help, we may come to believe that we can clearly determine what may be best for our clients. We may feel that what we do is in their best interest. It may lead us to "push" them into directions or behaviors that they would never consider and might not be appropriate at all for their life or development. This could move the client into a passive role as they seek to please the therapist or just want to be told what to do. If they could just be told what to do they would not be in our office. I am sure that there are many clients who have had lots of advice from well meaning "experts" on what they should be doing. We do not want to follow that pattern. We support our clients to make their own choices and decisions concerning what may be best for them.

Fourth, we do not want to get into debates with clients concerning labels. If a client comes in to the office and states, "I am an alcoholic", we will accept the frame of reference that they are working from without debate or disagreement. Labels can be useful to some persons and detrimental to others. It is not our place to label a client nor to get him or her to accept a label. Some labels may carry public stigma. If so, clients with healthy self-esteem would be most likely resistant to them. Any resistance will not help our cause. We are not looking for a power struggle. We are looking for internal client motivations to change. There seems to be no important advantage to labeling in therapy. Therefore, we must keep in our awareness that we wish to play down the urges to label behaviors and remove attention from them to enhance real motivation.

Fifth, our focus is on our client's concerns. If we become aware of other difficulties that we feel would be a more appropriate focus, we need to disregard our insights for the time being and allow the client to process as needed to develop their own conclusions. If we wish to focus on a different topic from our client, we are risking a struggle. The client is the expert. Allow things to develop in their frame of reference. If we see that a client would be better served by regression hypnosis and they simply wish to be treated for an addiction, we simply treat the addiction. It may come to light with motivational interviewing that the client will notice that something from the past is activating a trigger for their use. Then, we may simply offer additional services. This keeps the creative process of therapist/client interaction more productive.

Finally, counseling has a "no fault" policy. We do not want to get caught up in the "blame game". A client may enter treatment blaming their addiction on their past, their relationships, their anxiety, or many other factors. We can acknowledge this idea respectfully. However, blame is not important for our success. Treatment is not a court of law where we must lay blame or fault. Lots of needless time or energy may be wasted in seeking to make someone responsible. . "I would never have become this way if not for _____." We are here to treat the addiction that is currently troubling the client. We are seeking answers to be implemented in the now. We cannot erase the past. We cannot treat someone who is not present. We can simply reframe. "I cannot do anything about who is responsible for this happening to you. I can only help you decide what you are going to do about it."

Step by Step:
The One to Four Session
Hypnosis Model

Session 1: Assessment

This is the opportunity to begin to use your acquired motivational interviewing skills. Begin immediately after introducing yourself to the client to seek the answers to the questions regarding change and goals through your motivational interviewing techniques. Explore all events that recently led the client to seek treatment. Strive to use open ended questions and seek a total image of the life your clients are currently living and the life they desire to live. Remember, the clients are most likely ambivalent about change. Seek to compare and contrast these images while eliciting change talk. Discover the language and the goals you will use in directive hypnosis so that they will most approximate the exact image of the life your clients are seeking.

A good opening statement that includes the amount of time involved, the therapist's role, the client's role, some treatment goals, some details about hypnosis, and an open ended question will be most effective in getting things started.

"Our first session will last about 90 minutes. I want to get a deeper understanding of what brings you here. I'll probably spend a lot of time listening and gathering information. Then, I will be explaining and answering questions or concerns about hypnotherapy. Before we begin the therapy, I may need to ask some specific questions about details necessary for effective hypnosis. Now, tell me about your concerns over smoking?" Or, "Tell what has happened to bring you here for hypnotherapy today?" Something to this effect should get things started nicely.

Remember to affirm the client for coming in to see you. It takes courage to change. It takes courage to meet with a total stranger to discuss change. And, for many there are fears concerning hypnosis that must be overcome.

Now, the research has not established the selection criteria needed to determine whether or not to use hypnotic therapy. In the end, this will require the therapist's clinical judgment. However, a number of issues may need to be considered. Clients must be assessed for:

- Currently threatening suicide or homicide
- A recorded history of self injury or self mutilation that is currently active
- Exhibits psychosis, is out of touch with reality or actively hallucinating.
- Currently in an abusive relationship (either victim or perpetrator)
- Has history of any trauma (may require additional therapy)

These issues must be dealt with separately. The health and safety of the client, therapist, and others may well be at stake in some instances. If a prospective client meets these qualifying criteria, it is appropriate to move ahead with therapy. We need all information concerning any substance abuse/dependence disorder. We want to make sure we completely understand the extent of our client's use. This includes detailed historical information and current use patterns. We need to take measures to ensure their motivation is enhanced to the highest degree possible and that there are supports available for them in dealing with their substance use outside of our sessions. We want to verify that their home environment is stable. If they're homeless, living on the street, going through a divorce, or in an abusive home environment, this will clearly influence the therapy. It may be that now is just not the right time. We want to be sure of their emotional stability. The stressful nature of their environment may be too much and create an unstable mental health episode that will be detrimental to their ability to fully respond to the hypnotherapy. Again, our skills with motivational interviewing will also affect this situation and assist the client to be ready for change.

Of course, most importantly, we want to know if our clients are motivated to change. For this type of treatment, we need highly motivated individuals. If not, they may decide to leave treatment early on and not be able to eliminate their addictive behaviors. This may leave them at a lower level of functioning than before the treatment. We want to discuss the theory behind the treatment with a client in significant detail, educate them about it, and then allow them to make a well informed and reasonable decision concerning change. If any client has had a history of involvement in many treatment programs, it may be useful to examine previous records or contact prior therapists to find how well the client has previously engaged in treatment or how well he or she had participated in treatment. Prior success or failure with conventional therapies does not necessarily indicate the client will react the same now. However, it might be best used with clients who are in the appropriate stage of change as discussed earlier. Clients who have been well-informed about their problems while showing a dedication to improvement, possibly by demonstrating regular attendance and willingness to participate are often easiest to motivate.

Clients with personality disorder traits, particularly antisocial or borderline traits, are often not amenable to hypnotic therapies for addictions. Antisocial personality traits involve a pervasive pattern of behavior where the rights of others are disregarded or violated. This disorder is considered to be in evidence when a minimum of three of the following traits are exhibited: a) repeated performance of acts that are grounds for arrest, b) repeated deceit or lying, c) failure to plan ahead or impulsive behaviors, d) repeated physical fights or assaults, e) reckless disregard for the safety of self or others, f) repeated irresponsible behavior, such as failure to maintain work or honor financial obligations, or g) lack of remorse for harmful behavior to others.

Borderline personality traits involve a pervasive pattern of behavior demonstrating unstable interpersonal relationships, self image, and emotions, along with extremely impulsive behaviors. The disorder is considered to be exhibited with a minimum of five of the following traits: a) frantic efforts to avoid real or imagined abandonment, b) unstable and intense interpersonal relationships where the other is characterized by extremes of idealization and devaluation, c) unstable self image or sense of self, d) impulsivity in behaviors that become self-damaging (at least two of the following, i.e. sex, spending, substance abuse, reckless driving, or binge eating), d) recurring suicidal or self mutilating behavior, e) marked reactivity and instability of mood, f) chronic feelings of emptiness, g) inappropriate, intense anger, or h) transient, stress related paranoia or dissociation.

Any client demonstrating these traits will not be a good candidate for hypnotic addictions therapy without addressing these other issues. A person who has also experienced childhood or multiple traumas may develop PTSD, which might involve identification with a "victim" mythology where fear and safety dominate their lives and this is a possible deterrent to hypnosis for substance abuse as the client may be self medicating. In this case, the anxiety and/or PTSD must also be relieved or reduced along with the treatment for addiction. We would need to consider treatment for any co-morbid mental disorders.

Also, a poorly timed hypnotic intervention may be ineffective and increase resistance to treatment. Avoid clients who appear too omnipotent or have unstable ego boundaries if they do not seem to respond to seeking their own motivations. It may be that hypnosis may allow intense anger, shame, guilt, self-accusation, feelings of failure, and "What if?" thoughts to surface. Again, these are concerns that would need to be addressed further before dealing directly with the addiction issues.

Always, the client's motivations are the prominent issue. Intrinsic motivations will give us the results we require for lasting healthy change. And, addressing health, certainly, we need to get a physician's approval stating that the client is an appropriate candidate for therapy if there are

ANY health concerns that may affect treatment outcomes. For instance, someone with organic brain damage or other impairment might be a poor candidate for hypnotic therapy. To recap the selection criteria concerns involving clinical judgment include:

- Establish substance abuse status
- Screen for environmental stability
- Screen emotional stability and coping skills
- Suicide ideation
- Psychosis
- Determine the motivation level of client and stage of change
- Verify social support, cooperation, and problems
- Verify medical status (get medical release from physician if needed)

All treatment begins with a detailed assessment to determine if diagnosable substance abuse or dependence is actually present and if there are other clinical problems which might respond to hypnotherapy. If you feel uncomfortable in your abilities to assess substance use issues, it may be best to consult an alcohol and drug abuse professional who has specific training in this area before moving ahead. Again, this hypnotic treatment of addiction involves: enhancing motivation to change, ego strengthening, and directive hypnosis. The client may also have related problems such as anger, anxiety, depression, guilt, shame, or relationship issues. When considering motivational hypnosis therapy, the following conditions should be met: Clients must be capable of relaxation, following instructions from the therapists related to guided images, in relatively good health, have a stable home environment or strong social support, and be (or be capable of being) self motivated to stop abusing alcohol or drugs. It is not always necessary that clients be sober as the object is to increase sobriety as a direct result of the treatment.

A basic substance abuse/use assessment will consist of a client history related to ALL substance use including age of first use, feelings and memories related to first use, rewards for use (immediate and post), secondary gains (rewards related to use that are not a result of the chemical effects of the drug, i.e., social interactions, income, etc., costs of use both financial and personal, along with quantity and frequency of use. In cooperation with the client, we are seeking information and discovering motivations to change. I am always moving gently back and forth between what is desirable about use and what may not be. I may use an assessment tool such as the ASI (Addiction Severity Index), SASSI (Substance Abuse Subtle Screening Inventory) or the CAGE questionnaire in cases that involve the legal system or where a client's statements concerning use may be in doubt. These tools also provide more responses that may be reflected upon in such a way as to increase motivation to change. All assessment information is valuable to the treatment. Nothing is unimportant. Be alert for any clues the client reveals into possible avenues to sources of intrinsic motivation.

We need to discriminate here if the client is a user, abuser, or addicted (dependent). In substances, abuse is defined as continued use despite a failure to meet personal or professional obligations, use in environments that can be dangerous, negative interpersonal or legal consequences, or use of illegal substances and the risks that go along with this use. Dependence is characterized mainly by tolerance and withdrawal. Tolerance means that over time it takes more and more of the substance to get the same effects. Withdrawal indicates that there are negative physical consequences associated with discontinued use of the substance. Once it is determined whether the client is merely an abuser or actively in addiction or substance dependent, we will be able to estimate how many sessions are required. Many persons who are simply users or abusers may require only one treatment session with this protocol. For those who are substance dependent, I strongly suggest the therapist complete the entire 4 sessions with the client regardless.

Another factor that is helpful to explore is the family history of use and its consequences. The client may talk about the past or a well placed open ended approach such as, "What have been the patterns of _____ use in your family?" The strength of use in the family tree may be related to how easy or not the client may find their ability to quit. A strong family history of substance use difficulties will most likely indicate more than one session will be most effective in treatment.

In the appendix, I have included some simple tools that will be helpful in the assessment process. I have a sample of the simple intake and assessment form I often use. It can be copied or modified as appropriate for individual taste. These tools are not research based, thou some of the ideas and questions are definitely related to more elegant tools for assessment that do have scientific support, such as those mentioned previously. The chart for use over days of the week can assist to determine patterns that might be interrupted and triggers that may need to be displaced through the use of hypnosis (See chart of days Appendix 2). We can use a simple question to help us determine if the client is intrinsically or extrinsically motivated to enter treatment. I often ask, "What has brought you to seek to change this now?" If the clients respond by stating that they are required to be treated or they are doing this to make someone else happy, etc., then they are most likely going to require the full four session model. If the clients respond with, "I am here because I am ready to change" and gives a internal, personal reason for taking this action, then he they are probably ready for a one session treatment. Only a client who appears to be in "action" phase of change and is internally motivated is appropriate for a one session attempt. We must not allow the client who is not ready to attempt a one session treatment. If they fail once, they will expect failure. They will also tell other the treatment did not work and create expectations among future clients that they will not succeed in our program. Once the extent of substance use and the proposed number of sessions is determined, we can move into the scripting interview phase of our first session.

The one page assessment of values importance can also be helpful to assess exactly what the client might value most whether family, health, money, or spirituality, etc. This will also give the therapist fruitful information to explore with motivational interviewing techniques. There are many ways to use this simple picture/word assessment of values ratings, such as:

- How does your family relate to your behavior?
- What influence does your spiritual path play in this?
- How is your health affected by your actions?
- What happens to you financially afterwards?

These questions would be based on what the client rates as most important to them. Remember to reflect what you discover and seek statements for self change. These discoveries may be extremely important for scripting later.

We can influence the client's ability to talking about change for scripting with our interview. We need to look for signs of readiness to change in our client's answers. We can "test the waters" with questions such as, "What are you thinking you'd like to do about this?" or "Where does this leave you in terms of changing your _____?" or "What would have to be different for your life to improve?" Even if we clearly see where a change may be beneficial to the client, it is not our responsibility to offer suggestions for change. Leave responsibility to change with the clients! They are their own experts. They do not need us to tell them what to do. This is the heart of motivational interviewing and is very difficult for some persons who work in the substance abuse treatment field who may believe that they know what is best for addicted persons.

We are seeking to discover any hint of discomfort or disadvantage related to the current situation or behavior. We are investigating with our clients the possibilities of advantages to change. We hope to encourage optimism, confidence, and belief in the ability to change. Our clients have been successful before and need to be reminded of their strengths. If a client shares that they have never been successful at anything, I beg to differ. One might remind them of their ability to walk or any other obvious ability they express successfully. Finally, we are hoping for the client to express a strong intention of commitment to change. The client homework assignments, whether completed in office or at home, are focused on these topics.

The therapist may encourage sharing of information and change talk by inquiring about the clients anxieties, fears, or concerns surrounding making a change. We might even use a bit of self disclosure by sharing our own concerns about change. We will demonstrate nonjudgmental feedback or information sharing at all times to maintain an effective therapeutic relationship. We must keep alert to discover any signs of discomfort, interest, and ability to change while making mental notes of what might be most useful during hypnosis. Always, we seek to use reflections and summaries to draw out change talk

I tend to use guided relaxation for every first session. If the client is willing and seems a good candidate for hypnosis, it is very helpful to conduct a brief relaxation session to complete the intake. This allows the client to experience the positive aspects of the trance state and leave feeling as if something positive has occurred that they may take with them. I also give them a self hypnosis relaxation CD to use at their leisure. This assists them to practice between sessions and helps instill the ability to self relax within the clients. This is self empowering for the client and may aid in the future to resist cravings or urges. If the client seems very analytical or too stressed to respond well, I will send he or she home with the CD to practice alone prior to session 2.

Again, I will not risk failure and I want a positive trance experience in the office. If the client practices at home where comfortable and can enter trance, they are much more likely to be successful in their second office visit. If they are not successful, we can explore this further next visit and they may require specialized counting or confusion induction techniques. If the client is considered appropriate for one session. I will briefly cover all of the homework questions we have not explored during the intake and move directly into the hypnotic session (see Script in Appendix). However, if the client shows that they will need more sessions, he or she will be given the first homework assignment. If clients have completed an assessment tool such as the SASSI, I will forego homework and use the assessment as my guide for session two. Then, we shall utilize scripting based on the clients' replies to my open ended, motivational questions concerning their assessment responses. This will result in four sessions. If the homework is assigned during the first session, there will most likely only be three sessions.

The first homework consists of the first six worksheets in the appendix. You may decide to skip the pictures labeled "What is Important to Me?" as page 5 of the homework covers the same material in open question format. I often use both with some clients as it is most important to have a clear idea concerning the clients' values. The first sheet with pictures may be used to confirm or establish some basic values. In turn, these may be used to assess readiness or significant reasons to change.

For instance, a client rates their family as the #1, most important value in his or her life. We might simply ask how their use affects the family. The answer may lead the client to expand on how the use negatively impacts family life. This in turn may be used for scripting such as, "No longer causing discord in the family" or "Now, bringing the family together". These will depend on the client's responses but any item endorsed can be a topic for exploration by open ended questions.

Following this sheet, we have two assignments that may be completed during intake paperwork, if we are aware of the addiction issue and these might be appropriate as part of the assessment. One is "How much do you drink?" This can be very helpful to assess alcohol consumption, patterns, and challenges.

Next, we have an assignment sheet concerning the clients' current lifestyle. We are seeking to identify patterns that may be disrupted or replaced through hypnotherapy. We are asking clients to point out areas where change needs to happen. Any responses may be expanded and utilized for hypnosis scripting. For other addictions besides alcohol, or for alcohol if you prefer, the second sheet is appropriate. It is titled. "How much do you use?" The information obtained by this short questionnaire is valuable for assessment, motivational interviewing, and scripting. We may simply reword the form with, "How much do you gamble?" or "How often are you having sex?" In this way, the form can be modified to obtain valuable information for the treatment of many different addictions. Again, these may be used as part of the first session intake and assessment or they might be used as homework for session two. The choice is entirely up to the therapist. Any answers may be explored for motivations. Any answers may be used for scripting. Particularly, the questions, "What could be better?" and "What would you like to have happen as a result of hypnotherapy?" can elicit valuable information to assist treatment.

If the client is suitable for a one session treatment format, the therapist can pick and choose from the rest of the homework sheets any questions they believe will be valuable in assisting the hypnotherapy's success. I would complete the hypnotherapy used a standardized script much like the script in the appendix. The blanks in the script are to be completed with information from the motivational client interview. I always record the session using a digital recorder and immediately "burn" a CD of the session for the client to use at home if they feel they will need further reinforcement of the hypnosis. I prefer to use a sleep CD but I always ask the client if they would prefer a recording that instructs them to wake or sleep at the end. The clients are the experts on what is appropriate for them. I might suggest a sleep version if they ask for my opinion. I feel that using hypnosis recordings prior to sleep might last through the night and become more deeply imbedded. As of this writing, I am unaware if there is research to support or refute this theory. The one session client is now completed. I send them on their way with the CD and an open invitation to return if further, questions, concerns, or difficulties might arise.

For those clients who appear to require a more intense therapeutic experience, especially those who are truly in addiction or dependence and not simply abusers or habitual behavior repeaters, I assign the first homework sheets to be completed and returned the following session. If I am reasonably sure that the client will not respond well to hypnosis without some practice, I will assign the simple values and use sheets along with an induction/relaxation CD (about 15 minutes). My main hope is that they will practice relaxing into trance before the second session. Then with the first simple assignments we will complete our beginning MI and hypnosis in the second session.

The Second Session

The focus of the second session is determined by the results of the first. Of course, if clients were appropriate for a single session and seemed satisfied with their hypnosis, there will be no second session for them. Second sessions are for those who require intensive motivational work.

To begin, we simply do a counseling check in with the clients. We would need to explore the effects of self relaxation homework with the assigned CD. After checking in with the clients, we would process any documented assessment tools. I find that any answers to any valid assessment may be expanded upon by reframed open ended questions to elicit motivational responses. For instance, a "yes" answer to "have you ever felt guilty after using?" This response could be approached with a simple, "Tell me more about that." This could reveal a treasure trove of motivations to quit.

Next, we would examine responses to the basic homework assignments of: *What is Important to Me?; How Much do I Drink?; or How much Do I Use?* We must make note of any information that will be useful for change in our hypnosis scripting. Then we are ready for our first motivational hypnotherapy approach as we integrate clients' response into their hypnosis for change.

Once the hypnosis is completed, we check in with the client and process anything of importance or note, especially any thoughts related to inspirations or intuitions about improved change. Again, we are seeking intrinsic motivations to change that may enhance or improve our next session. Once this process is completed to our mutual satisfaction, we will begin to explain and discuss the motivational homework for session three.

The homework for session three consists of very basic motivational assignments. We are asking the client to explore their current lifestyle, schedule, or daily/weekly routine. We hope to discover outlines of behavior that can be interrupted or replaced by more healthy patterns. Insist that the client tell you what works for them and what needs to change. We want healthy and pleasing activities to increase. These assignments are in Appendix 2 and begin with Current vs. Future Lifestyle. Assign all worksheets from this beginning assignment through the Future Intention assignment. This will include the costs and benefits of changing vs. staying the same and another important values worksheet. All five worksheets need to be completed for session three. Remember you may decide to proceed directly to session three homework following the first session if you desire to do so and it seems appropriate for the client. This would be using a three session approach.

Session 3: Change, Values, & Intentions

We simply begin with a check in as in all sessions. If the assigned worksheets are not completed, we may elect to continue and complete the sheets in session or cancel until the worksheets are completed. I decide depending on my schedule. However, it should be noted that if a client does not complete the worksheets it may indicate a lack of true motivation to make changes. If there is any intuition that this is what is occurring, the session should be cancelled until the client demonstrates willingness to complete the assignments.

If the homework is in order, we want to identify routines that are not so healthy or cause clients difficulty. We need information on how the clients' routine affects their health, finances, relationships, and achievements. We are always seeking change talk. The clients may tell us how could life can be better and what would have to change for this to take place.

The next assignments have to do with cause/effects. What will be the results of staying the same vs. change? Other programs use different terms that you might find more appropriate such as what is good vs. not so good or what is desirable vs. undesirable about your addiction or behavior? I simply use a cost vs. benefit approach. Any of these approaches will work. We avoid using positive vs. negative or good vs. bad terminology as this can snare us into confrontation or taking sides. The object here is for the client to make a concrete record of the influences that result from the addiction. Some clients may argue that there is no benefit to use. Gently remind them that if there was no benefit, the use would never have continued. We must be honest with ourselves. If I smoke to reduce stress, then stress reduction is a benefit. The next question would be, what are some other ways I might enjoy relieving stress that are healthier for me? We must seek out the motivation or stimulus for life improvement. There are some listed areas to cover be sure to address each with open questioning, just in case the client did not fully explore his or her answers. How is your health affected by your _____? What type of legal issues have resulted or might result in your future from your _____ ? How does _____ help your relationship? What are the good things that happen after _____? What happens that is not so good? I try to seek the benefits for the behavior first and end on the costs. I feel that the most recent or last thoughts concerning the behavior will remain in the client's consciousness longer, especially if they are not desirable.

We are working here to overcome ambivalence and shift the decisional balance in favor of change. Normalize the clients' ambivalence. You might even explain ambivalence and the approach/avoidance conflicts here and how all persons are affected by them. The written list helps to quantify the answers in column form. Sometimes, this makes the decision to change easier as the list in favor of change may be far larger than if the list in favor of staying the same is the greatest. Asking more open ended questions here to determine the "force" exerted on the client's behavior by the many pros and cons listed will also be helpful. Information on why use is attractive to the client is helpful to establish rapport and search for other activities that can replace the behavior. This is a very important set of exercises.

Next, we would cover the client's values. This may be somewhat redundant to the earlier picture assignment, "What is Important to Me?'" However, I discovered that this assignment can uncover values that might be missed by the simpler "ratings" version. Here, we ask the clients to brainstorm a list of values and traits that are important to their core beliefs and improved self esteem. We ask them to then identify the two most important. This is similar to self image/self esteem work. We are hoping the client has an "ideal" image of who they can be. Then, we ask how they can become more in line with their values. The benefit is two-fold, decreased addiction and improved self esteem. No one can decide this for the client. After all this you might conclude by asking, "No one can tell you what to do. Knowing all of this, what would you like to have happen?" This will lead to the next and last homework sheet.

Finally, for session three, the last assignment has encouraged the client to look to the future. We seek to know the clients' hopes and dreams for the future. We want to clearly understand how these hopes and dreams are important to our clients. We are seeking to view their futures through their vision, not our own. We might encourage the client to brainstorm and create a list of options for the future. Then, they might decide which suits their needs best. It is vital the clients examine current behaviors and the relationship between current actions and likelihood of their success. Some current actions may lead to success and we want to develop those. This is simple to integrate into hypnosis scripting. The clients may be instructed to increase any behavior or simply notice that they are enjoying doing it more frequently. Some things the clients have been doing are detrimental to their dreams. We want to identify these barriers and remove them. They may be pleasantly surprised to notice that those behaviors simply disappear. We guide the clients to describe activities that they would like to become involved in that would be helpful to replace the time spent on less helpful actions/behaviors and increase the likelihood of making their dreams come true. Once we have gathered our clients' answers from all of these sources, the scripting consists of simply inserting suggestions to reinforce their choices during hypnosis. Be careful to use the clients' own words rather than your reflections. Mostly, their own language is more easily accepted. However, if you reflect to the client by using images or metaphors and the client responds enthusiastically to them, by all means use them during hypnosis. Following the clients' reorientation from hypnosis, process any feelings, questions, or concerns. Then, move immediately into explaining the last set of client homework and closing this session. The last session is concerned with client self efficacy. We want to create the success mindset by focusing on clients' perceived strengths and previous successes. We want to have the client create a concrete, intentional change plan while rating their confidence, enthusiasm, and anticipation concerning the change. Then we simply use hypnosis to suggest the way strengths may be used for current success while directing the client to take the steps they propose.

Final Session: Self -Efficacy, Intention, and Plan for Success

The final session puts everything together. All of the information that you have gathered from the previous sessions needs to be gathered together, combined with current assignments, and offered in a powerful closing hypnotherapy session. The client may be well into change by now. The idea is that victory over the addiction is assured. Faith is the treatment should be strong. When checking in with the client at the beginning of the session, start with a question statement such as, "Tell me about your successes". The focus is to be success.

I want to take a moment here to explain my ideas around intention. Back when I trained graduate interns in counseling, I would mention intention and some of my interns would look at me with a blank expression and ask, "What do you mean Intention?" Intention has been defined in many ways. It is a plan of action or an aim that guides an action. It is also known as what something is meant to convey; a meaning or concept o something. In the medical field, intention describes the course or manner of healing a surgical wound. In a sense, this is an aim of repair. In Latin, the word was *intentio,,* meaning to stretch toward (from *intendere*).

Intention has taken on a variety of connotations recently such as an aim that causes us to grow, an active force in the universe, a force acting on the quantum field, or possibly Consciousness itself. I like to think of intention as **the art of aligning our consciousness with infinite consciousness in order to become co-creators of our realty.** This may seem pretentious but it conveys the true power of having an intention towards change.

What if all our clients had ever thought about was what they could not do or what was missing from their lives? Now, suddenly, the opportunity is right in front of them to change but they have no clear intentions. What are they to grow toward? What is the goal? This is beyond their addictions. This is what will move them into the final stage of transcendence. Suppose up until now the client has been consumed with thoughts of how he or she doesn't like where they are or, how things can never change, they have always been this way. Consider the clients who have believed that they had no choices and must, should, or have to behave as they have in the past so that others will accept them (apologies to Albert Ellis).

We are asking them to choose again. We are seeking to plant the seed of belief in the clients that they can attract, move, change, and choose a new life. Suddenly, they are confronted with this frightening freedom. Someone once said, if you change the way you look at things and the things you look at change. Staying the same is safe. Ambivalence exists because of this. It is easy to turn back without a clear intention, goal, and plan.

In this session, it is critical to assist the clients in their ability to become clear and focused. The clients need to know what they really want. They require a plan for their greatest good and the good of all concerned. This session is the clarification of these things and all that has been revealed in sessions before.

Following is a list of questions that may help. You can use these inquiries in earlier sessions at any appropriate time. You will note that they may parallel earlier work. If these have not been answered before, now is the time. The clients must ask themselves some questions that might promote this intention thinking, such as:

- If you were your "ideal" self, what kind of person would you be and what traits would you have?
- What would you be doing if you lived as you wanted to?
- What seems to be missing from life or what might you not be getting?
- What appears to stop you or gets in your way?
- What are you doing now to create the life what you want?
- What did you actually do this past week?
- What did you want to do differently this past week?
- What stopped you from doing what you say you want to do?
- What will you do tomorrow? Next week?
- How is what you are doing NOW helpful or harmful to you?
- What are you doing that you really want?
- How are your actions working for you?
- How does what you are doing match your beliefs?
- How committed are you to change?

You may even want to assign these questions early on or simply pick and choose from them to ask during sessions to augment your ability to improve motivations. They are intention seeking in nature.

The homework should be approached in the same manner as all previous work. The client response should be expanded upon through the use of open-ended motivational questions. Our first sheet is the focus on past successes. We are going to support self efficacy and expectation for success. What ever the intention for change, the seed for triumph begins with an empowered client. We are seeking evidence of ability. We are seeking self pride. The clients' beliefs about their abilities will be revealed and their strengths promoted.

The first of the assignments is asking the client to recall a past success. I have actually been confronted with some difficulties here. Many of my clients have been absolutely convinced that they have never been successful at anything. I use examples of two or three instances of success with good effect. One example I use concerning successes is for the client to consider sperm. When their parents were having sex, they were nothing until a sperm reached the egg. Sperm count can be in the low millions to over 360 million. That is one large race. Anyone living has a part of them that has won that race. The strongest, fastest, and most successful sperm will win. If that is too abstract, I ask them to consider walking. If they are able to walk, they have been successful. They did not fall down and decide for themselves, "Hey, this crawling is cool. I think I will just crawl for the rest of my life because walking is just too difficult." Would we just quit? A walker is determined and successful. If we have the simple drive of a 7 to 12 month old about any undertaking, we will prevail. Last, I may use talking. The ability to communicate verbally is very complicated. It is also something most of us were determined to accomplish. Is the client a failure at talking? Any of these can be helpful to break the "failure mind". I am sure that a creative therapist can think of many more examples to use.

So, we set the scene for success. Examine the assignment. The client should have listed some positive changes he or she has made at some time in life. Then, they were to choose one of the changes, maybe the one that was hardest to accomplish or they felt most proud of, and examine how they accomplished this change. Was it all at once? Did it take some time, steps, and planning? We want to know how they did it. We want to emphasize their abilities and minimize difficulties as having been conquered. We want to determine what prompted them to act. We identify their thoughts and the environment that promoted their motivation. Finally, we want them to tell us their current thoughts and feelings about the changes they made. Use any relevant success information to enhance belief in ability now.

The strengths exercise will help us to increase client self esteem and expectation of triumph over addiction. Sometimes clients can get stuck in negative thought patterns, forgetting their accomplishments. We need to remind them of the ways in which they are personally strong and powerful. By first acknowledging their past successes, this may be easier to do. The exercise asks them to list their personal strengths and strong points. The focus of these first exercises is gaining self-efficacy and self esteem. As they spotlight their empowering traits, we seek to aid them in identifying how these traits will enable them to change their addictive behavior effectively. We also want to identify and plan for barriers that may hinder progress. The clients can develop ideas about how their empowering traits will aid them in removing any obstacles they confront on their journey through change.

Next, we will examine the concrete plan of the client's future intention. This is a standard plan adapted from Miller and Rollnick (1998). The clients are asked to list specific areas or ways in which they want to change. They report specific goals or targets. They need to include positive goals to begin creating change, increasing positive behaviors, and expectations for improvements or modifications of behavior. The detail to which this is completed will often indicate the seriousness with which the client approaches the change. If the plan seems to be ill prepared or vague, it is not inappropriate to guide the client through open questions to a more detailed plan.

It is critical that the clients identify the most important reason(s) for wanting these changes to take place. These may have been formulated during their decisional balance work, when clients determined the most likely results of changing vs. staying the same.

We uncover the reasons for changing that are the most significant for clients and those close to them. Hopefully, the clients have also considered the emotional consequences of changing. We require specific steps in this plan to change. We need beginning actions that may be accomplished quickly and long term goals. The clients must be specific on how, when, and where they will make these steps happen. We also need to recognize the specific ways other people can aid and support the clients. Help the clients to identify who they will seek out to assist and support their intentions. Be sure they list specific ways that others (friends, family, counselors, etc.) can help support them in their endeavors to change.

A good plan must be capable of being evaluated. Clients must know how they will determine if their intention is working. How will the clients be able to measure if these favorable outcomes manifest? The clients will describe their expectations of what will happen as a consequence of the change. There should be clear advantages that they will obtain from changing. A proposal for how they know they are successful needs to be in place.

It is important to recognize specific obstacles that may be encountered. If identified, any events that may slow clients down or get in the way can be circumvented. It is important to anticipate any situations or difficulties that might possibly need to confronted. It is much easier to stick with a plan regardless of obstacles and delays if preparations for difficulties are completed in advance. The idea is to navigate obstacles and reach our destination. It will be helpful for the clients to list steps towards problem solution or reorganizing strategies that they would use. Also, it is good to identify those they would approach for assistance is needed.

Finally, the client is asked to use a simple rating scale to determine the importance of this change in their life, the confidence they have concerning their abilities, and their emotional evaluation of the change. I have a worksheet of questions that the client may answer but it is best if the therapist asks these questions based on the client's ratings. We need to use these scales to reinforce our final determination of the client's motivation and use them to make final adjustments in our efforts to enhance movement towards change.

If the client has marked less than a "5" rating on the Importance scale and it is not a zero, then why is the rating not lower? Why is it not a zero or a number lower? Ask the client to explain as best he or she can. We need to identify how could it become more important? What could improve the rating? What would have to happen to move the rating up just one more? What would make it become a "5"? Repeat this process with each scale. If the client has marked less than a "5" rating on the Confidence scale and it is not a zero, then why is the rating not lower? Why is it not a zero or a number lower? Ask the client to explain. How could it become more important? What could improve the rating? What would have to happen to move the rating up just one more? What would make it become a "5"? Lastly, if the client has marked less than a "5" rating on the Desire scale and it is not a zero, then why is the rating not lower? Why is it not a zero or a number lower? Ask the client to explain. How could it become more important? What could improve the rating? What would have to happen to move the rating up just one more? What would make it become a "5"? Following this gathering of information, we have only to complete the final hypnosis session. We may now put it all together and insert the material into our hypnosis script.

CLOSING THOUGHTS

As with basic motivational interviewing, the time has come to summarize all that has been revealed by the assignments. Like a careful arrangement of picked flowers, the fruit of these labors must be gifted back to the clients. We have been working with creative scripting each session. The clients have most likely given us appropriate feedback as to what appears to be effective and what is not. We now have the intention plan mapped out and can give concise suggestions to target the exact manner in which the clients wish to direct their efforts. We also have the barriers to change identified. We insert simple ideas for their removal along the way into our words. The clients are most likely in a powerfully charged state of intrinsic motivation.

We begin as with all hypnotherapy sessions by ensuring the environment is quiet, safe, and comfortable. Before proceeding, check in with the clients' energy and mood. You may need to gently remind them of their ratings of importance, confidence, and desire. Remind them that feelings are always guides. Positive emotions concerning the change will act as magnets that draw the client towards the desired outcome. Use your preferred induction and maybe insert a specific statement of the intention. The script provided allows for mental rehearsal with vivid detail of the established intention and the feelings of success to be experienced. I might add in the end a statement of detachment such as, "This or something better will be." We do not want to sabotage the possibility that whatever we have determined from our sessions, something even better can manifest itself in the clients' world.

Finally, I have developed an acronym that I use as my guide through all hypnotic endeavors. This simple five letter reminder is AIMSS ©. If the aim is true we shall not miss the target.

AIMSS stands for:
- **A – Attainable**
- **I – Involve positive emotions**
- **M – Measurable**
- **S - Keep It Simple**
- **S – Senses**

AIMSS © (copyright protected)

We ensure the goals are attainable, involve the clients' positive emotions, make sure outcomes can be measured, keep the suggestions simple, and involve all five senses. If these requirements are met, there can be no failure. There will be change. The final touch is detachment from specifics. We have been very specific in our work. However, the freedom to allow the unconscious to express change in the way that is best for the client cannot be understated. The client knows what is best, always.

All of our conscious efforts and all of the clients' conscious efforts still rely on the unconscious mind. The resources are within the client to make the changes necessary for the good of all concerned. The seeds of thought have been planted. The motivation creates the environment for fertile growth. The unconscious is the driving, all knowing force.

When the hypnosis is completed, we process the clients' experiences. We summarize the therapy session with an expectation of success. Then, we say goodbye. The goal all along is to empower the client. They are free to experience the triumph of their own work. They can move on with stronger ego strength and improved self esteem with expectations of continued success.

The MI and hypnosis approaches described here are based on the work of others. This unique combination is my own. The evidence to date for both methods of treatment is very encouraging. We are just beginning to understand. I am hopeful that the clinicians who use this approach will further research into the combinations of these two techniques in a creative and open manner that is helpful to us all. The ultimate goal here is being able to assist more clients in the improvement of their lives.

References

Allison, D. B., & Faith, M. S. (1996). Hypnosis as an adjunct to cognitive-behavioral psychotherapy for obesity: A meta-analytic reappraisal. *Journal of Consulting and Clinical Psychology, 64*(3), 513-516.

Burke, B.L., Arkowitz, H., & Menchola, M. (2003). The efficacy of motivational interviewing: A meta-analysis of controlled clinical trials. *Journal of Consulting and Clinical Psychology, 71(5),* 843-861.

Carels, R. A., Darby, L., Cacciapaglia, H. M., Konrad, K., Coit, C., Harper, J., et al. (2007). Using motivational interviewing as a supplement to obesity treatment: A stepped-care approach. *Health Psychology, 26*(3), 369-374.

Chips, A. (1999). *Clinical Hypnotherapy: A Transpersonal Approach.* Goshen, VA: EIH Publishing.

Crasilneck, H. B. (1990). Hypnotic techniques for smoking control and psychogenic impotence. *American Journal of Clinical hypnosis, 32,* 147-153.

DiClemente, C. C. (1981). Self efficacy and smoking cessation maintenance a preliminary report. *Cognitive Therapy and Research, 5,* 175-187.

Dunn, E. C., Neighbors, C., & Larimer, M. E. (2006). Motivational Enhancement Therapy and Self-Help Treatment for Binge Eaters. *Psychology of Addictive Behaviors, 20*(1), 44-52.

Egan, G. (1982). *The Skilled Helper: A Model for systematic helping and Interpersonal Relating (2nd Ed.).* Monterey, CA: Brooks-Cole.

Havens, R. A., & Walters, C. (2002). *Hypnotherapy scripts: A Neo-Ericksonian Approach for Persuasive Healing* (2nd ed.). New York: Brunner-Routledge.

Hutchinson-Phillips, S., & Gow, K. (2005). Hypnosis as an adjunct to CBT: Treating self-defeating eaters. *Journal of Cognitive and Behavioral Psychotherapies, 5*(2), 113-138.

Kirsch, I., Montgomery, G., & Sapirstein, G. (1995). Hypnosis as an adjunct to cognitive-behavioral psychotherapy: a meta-analysis. *Journal of Consulting and Clinical Psychology, 63,* 214-220.

Lynn, J.L., Neufeld, V., Rhue, J.W., & Matorin, A. (1993). Hypnosis and smoking cessation: A cognitive behavioral treatment. In J.W. Rhue, S.J. Lynn, & I. Kirsch (Eds*.) Handbook of Clinical Hypnosis*. (pp. 555-585). Washington, DC: American Psychological Association.

Miller, W. (Eds.). (1980). *The Addictive Behaviors: Treatment of Alcoholism, Drug Abuse, Smoking, and Obesity.* New York: Pergamon Press.

Miller, W., & Rollnick, S. (1998). *Motivational Interviewing: Preparing People for Change* (1st ed.). New York: Guilford Press.

Miller, W., & Rollnick, S. (2002). *Motivational Interviewing: Preparing People for Change* (2nd ed.). New York: Guilford Press.

Morris, W. (Ed). (1982). *The American Heritage Dictionary of the English Language (New College Edition)*. Boston: Houghton Mifflin.

Nigg, C. R., Burbank, P. M., Padula, C., Dufresne, R., Rossi, J. S., Velicer, W. F., et al. (1999). Stages of change across ten health risk behaviors for older adults. *The Gerontologist, 39*(4), 473-482.

Perry, C., Gelfand, R., & Marcovitch, P. (1979). The relevance of clinical susceptibility in the clinical context. *Journal of Abnormal Psychology, 88,* 592-603.

Pederson, L. L., Scrimgeour, W. G., & Lefcoe, N. M. (1975).
Comparison of hypnosis plus counseling, counseling alone, and
hypnosis alone in a community service smoking withdrawal
program. *Journal of Consulting and Clinical Psychology, 43,*
920.

Prochaska, J. O., & DiClemente, C. C. (1983). Stages and processes of
self-change of smoking: Toward an integrative model of change.
Journal of Consulting and Clinical Psychology, 51(3), 390-395.

Prochaska, J.O., DiClemente, C.C. & Norcross, J.C. (1992). In search of
how people change: Applications to addictive behaviors.
American Psychologist, 47(9), 1102-1114.

Prochaska, J. O., Norcross, J.C., & DiClemente, C.C. (1994). *Changing
For Good: A Revolutionary Six-Stage Program for Overcoming
Bad Habits and Moving Your Life Positively Forward.* New
York: Harper Collins.

Prochaska, J.O., Velicer, W.F., Rossi, J.S., Goldstein, M.G., Marcus,
B.H., Rakowski, W., Fiore, C., Harlow, L.L., Redding, C.A.,
Rosenbloom, D., & Rossi, S.R. (1994). Stages of change and
decisional balance for twelve problem behaviors. *Health
Psychology, 13*(1), 39-46.

Rogers, C. (1951). *Client Centered Therapy.* Boston: Houghton Mifflin.

Rogers, C. (1959). A theory of therapy, personality and interpersonal
relationships, as developed in the client-centered framework. *In
S. Koch (Ed.), Psychology: A study of science,* (Vol. 3, pp. 210-
211; 184-256). New York: McGraw Hill.

Rogers, C. (1961). *On Becoming A Person.* Boston: Houghton Mifflin.

Sarkin, J. A., Johnson, S. S., Prochaska, J. O., & Prochaska, J. M. (2001).
Applying the Transtheoretical Model to regular moderate
exercise in an overweight population: Validation of a stages of

change measure. *Preventive Medicine: An International Journal Devoted to Practice and Theory, 33(5)*, 462-469.

Tang, S., & Hall, V. C. (1995). The over-justification effect: A meta-analysis. *Applied Cognitive Psychology, 9*, 365-404.

Truax, C.B. & Carkhuff, R.R. (1967). *Toward Effective Counseling and Psychotherapy. Chicago: Aldine.*

Truax, C.B. & Mitchell, K.M. (1971). Research on certain therapist interpersonal skill in relation to process and outcome. In A.E. Bergin & S.L. Garfield (Eds*.) Handbook of Psychotherapy and Behavior Change: An Empirical Analysis.* (pp. 299-344). New York: Wiley.

Valle, S.K. (1981). Interpersonal functioning of alcoholism counselors and treatment outcome. *Journal of Studies on Alcohol, 42, 783-790.*

Van Nuys, D. (1975). On the phrasing of hypnotic suggestions: a brief case report. *Psychotherapy: Theory, Research, and Practice, 12,* 302-304.

Appendix 1 – Basic Motivational Script

You know NOW you want to stop _____. You now know that it is your decision to stop _____. And you also now know, that you can, you will, you must do exactly what you must do to stay away from any & all _____. You also NOW know, that you can, you will, you must do exactly what you must do to finally bury this addiction (or _____) before the addiction buries you. As you know, you will only ever have one body, one life for this body, only one mind, unique together in each and every way. The time is now to love for your body. The one & only body you will ever have deserves love and care. The time is NOW to add years of health and add health to your years. As a new healthy, happy, and refreshed non – _____. That's right. Years of health and health to your years. Becoming a healthy happy, & relaxed person. You know NOW you want to stop _____. You now know that it is your decision to stop _____. And you also now know, that you can, you will, you must do exactly what you must do to stay away from any & all _____. Your new inner commitment is to be free. Doing exactly what you must do day after day, after day to be a non-_____and feel good. You add years of health and add health to your years. That's right, add years of health and add health to your years. Doing exactly what you must do to finally bury this addiction (or _____) before the addiction buries you. Being the new happy, healthy non- _____ you.

Now use your god given creative imagination to see yourself going about your daily (evening, weekend, _____) routine without _____. Getting up in the morning, preparing for the day, having breakfast, coffee, tea, juice, or whatever you choose to have while forgetting to even think about _____. See yourself wherever you might go without a care or thought about this _____. Notice how good you feel. Free and clean, breathing deeply from the fresh air. You go through each and every day, day after day, after day, without _____ and feeling good. Going through your evening activities without _____. Very relaxed and tranquil. Peaceful and easy feeling. Filled with Love, (love for God), love for your family, love for your body. The one & only body you will ever have deserves love and care. No longer poisoning your body with _____. Doing exactly what you must do day after day, after day to be healthy and feel good. You add years of health and add health to your years. That's right, add years of health and add health to your years. Finally burying this addiction (or _____) before the addiction buries you.

Now take another nice, long, slow deep breath. With each breath you take, simply allow your self to go deeper into relaxation. You may notice that the sound of my voice becomes more relaxing to you. You may notice that the sound of the music becomes more and more relaxing to you. You may notice that sounds outside of the room become more relaxing to you. As you gently drift deeper with each breath, you let the following thoughts and ideas enter deep into your inner mind and become part of your life in the form of permanent behaviors. So that once and for all how you think, how you feel and how you behave is living the life of a non-_____. You want to be a non-_____. It is your decision to quit forever. For this moment forward, you will stop _____ for the rest of your life. You never want to _____ again under any circumstances. Doing exactly what you must do day after day, after day to be healthy and feel good. You add years of health and add health to your years. That's right, add years of health and add health to your years. Burying this addiction (or _____) before the addiction buries you.

[If using a home self hypnosis follow up CD]

[Please exhale now and take another nice, long, slow deep breath. May I remind you to simply use your CD in bed at night, over and over and over again. Again, use your CD in bed at night in bed at night every night over and over and over again for at least the next twenty-one nights. This will simply remove any and all desires for_____. Finally controlling the one and only you that you will ever have and putting yourself in charge. Putting you in charge of your own inner success that you possessed from birth. Doing exactly what you must do day after day, after day to be healthy and feel good. You add years of health and add health to your years. That's right, add years of health and add health to your years. Burying this addiction (or _____) before the addiction buries you.]

That's right! Finally, doing what you say you want to do. Knowing you are doing exactly what you say you will do, what you must do day after day, after day to be healthy and feel good. You add years of health and add health to your years. That's right, add years of health and add health to your years. Burying this addiction (or _____) before the addiction buries you.

Exhale.

Relax.   Just Let Go.

[Motivational inserts] Up until NOW, you thought that you needed _____ for (LIST positive or "Good Things"). But now you know that you never needed _____ for any of those things. From this moment forward, _____ has nothing to do with _____(list). _____. You can also now think back on all the problems and frustrations with this addiction, you realize it had nothing to do with the good person you are. You simply feel more and more positive and grateful that you are moving beyond this block in your life now. Now you're reaching an awareness...that _____has *nothing to do* with _____(list +).

That's right. Because NOW you are remembering vividly all of the problems and difficulties that are not so good about _____. You can remember all of the _____(list – stuff) and KNOW that you never have to feel that way again. And, you don't know when you'll ever _____ again. Because NOW you are free. FREE to forget all about this addiction. It can be erased from your mind. You can think those old thoughts that bring you down or make you upset. But, I think you will find something very interesting has now happened. And, your unconscious mind can be in control. So you find your self thinking about more positive things, joyful things, interesting things that you would rather think about or do, new ways of being active, happy, and social. So you forget to even think about _____.

The longer you stay away from _____ the better you will feel. Focusing on your future. On your goals. On the changes you are making for the good. Such as, (Homework)

_____

_____Day after day after day feeling more happy, more content, more in control. Feeling healthier, more calm, more refreshed, more relaxed. From this moment forward, completely refreshed, completely relaxed. Doing exactly what you must do day after day, after day to be healthy and feel good. You add years of health and add health to your years. That's right, add years of health and add health to your years. Burying this addiction before the addiction buries you.

Any and all desires for_____ are simply disappearing. What you have wanted to do is now done. Your new desires for _____ (goals for success) are where you are headed now. Fulfilling your dreams and desires for a healthy, wonderful life. Just exhale, relax, enjoy, let go……. FREE. SUCCESS. HEALTHY. HAPPY.

Once more, using your unlimited and powerful imagination. Simply be, simply imagine the successful you, going throughout your days, at work, at home, or at play, the new healthy, happy, clean, pure, refreshed, and relaxed you. Feel how good it is to be that way forever. Please imagine this now.

(REORIENT).

Appendix 2: Motivational Handouts and Forms

To be used with clients to enhance motivation to change. These may also be used to create directive scripts for change.

Client: _____Date: _____

Identifying Information: (Age, race, physical description, etc.)

Appearance:	Speech:	Motor Activity:	Affect:	*Mood*
__ Well Groomed	__ Normal	__ Calm	__ Normal	*Score*:
__ Disheveled	__ Soft	__ Agitated	__ ***Depressed***	(1 to 10)
__ Malnourished	__ Loud	__ Hyperactive	__ ***Anxious***	
__ Obese	__ Pressured	__ Hypoactive	__ Flat	_____
	__ Rapid	__ Tremors	__ Angry	
			__ Elated	
			__ Labile	
			__ Inappropriate	

Thought Process:	Judgment:	Insight:	Memory:	Orientation:
__ Lucid/Coherent	__ Intact	__ Intact	__ Intact	__ Oriented X3
__ Loose	__ Limited	__ Limited	__ Impaired	__ Disoriented
__ Tangential	__ Impaired	__ Impaired		
__ Other				

** Has client ever had thoughts of harming self or others? When? Explain.

Presenting Problem (State first in client's own words why they are here; What/When, etc.):

Family/Social History (Divorce, parents, step-parents, siblings, home, alcohol or drug use in family tree, etc.):

Education/Employment History:

Medical/Psychiatric/Counseling History:

Client Strengths/Resources:

Substance Use History:

Substance   Age of 1st use   Quantity then & now   Frequency then & now

Alcohol- drink____drunk____   _____   _____

Marijuana-   _____   _____   _____

Other drugs (list all reported):

_____   _____   _____
_____   _____   _____
_____   _____   _____

Past 30 Days: ____ drinking ____ drunk ____ marijuana _____other

Last Day Used: Alcohol _____ Quantity _____
                   Marijuana _____ Quantity _____
Others _____

Checklist SA or SD:

___ increased tolerance ___attempts to control/ quit ___ financial problems

____ driven intoxicated ____ DIP/DUI ____ Hospital/ER visit

___blackouts...How often ? _____How long?_____ Last? _____

___Driving: accidents ____ loss of license ___ TX_____

___Annoyed by concern of others____ Felt guilty (drinking or behavior)

Are you concerned by your drinking or use? _____

Legal Charges : _____

Probation _____ Name of PO and location: _____
Assessment and Recommendations: (Suicide or homicide ideation ___)

Counselor signature, title, and date:_____

WHAT IS IMPORTANT TO ME?
(Please rate #1 – 10)

 Money  Career  **Health**

 Education  Self Respect/Trust

 Freedom  Family  Spirituality

 Friends My Substance Use

How much do you drink*?

SUN	MON	TUES	WED	THUR	FRI	SAT	TOTAL

(*One drink equals; a 12 oz beer, about one shot of liquor, or a typical glass of wine)

Binge drinking questions:

For Men: In the past two weeks, how many times have you had 5 or more drinks in one day/setting? _____

For Women: In the past two weeks, how many times have you had 4 or more drinks in one day/setting? _____

Both:

How many times have you consumed alcohol in the past month (estimate)? _____

How many times have you consumed alcohol in the past year (estimate)?   _____

How much do you spend on alcohol per Week?   Month?   Year?

Have you ever felt guilty about something that happened while drinking?
Yes ___   No ___

Have you ever taken a drink the morning after to feel better? Yes ___ No ___

Has anyone told you that they were concerned or annoyed you about your drinking?
Yes ___   No ___

Have you ever felt you should cut down or limit your drinking? Yes ___ No __

How much do you use*?

SUN	MON	TUES	WED	THUR	FRI	SAT	TOTAL

(*Determine a standard amount of any substance in cooperation. For instance, a pack of cigarettes)

How old were you when you stared to use? _____ What was it like? _____

_____

How is it now?_____

_____

_____

How many times per day do you use_____ ?   _____

How many in the past month (estimate)? _____

How many times in the past year (estimate)?   _____

How does this make you feel? _____

_____

_____

What could be better? _____

_____

_____

How much do you spend on _____ per Week?   Month?   Year?

Have you ever felt guilty about your use? Yes ____   No ____ How come?

_____

_____

Has anyone told you that they were concerned or annoyed you about your use?
Yes ____   No ____

What would you like to have happen as a result of hypnotherapy? _____

_____

_____

CURRENT VS. FUTURE LIFESTYLES

Your routine can affect your health (physical and mental), finances, relationships, and achievements. To examine your lifestyle NOW, please complete the following timeline describing your daily activities on a "typical day." Remember to include times when you might be involved in activities or behaviors you wish to change. Then answer the questions.

7am _____	5pm _____
8am _____	6pm _____
9am _____	7pm _____
10am _____	8pm _____
11am _____	9pm _____
Noon _____	10pm _____
1pm _____	11pm _____
2pm _____	Midnight _____
3pm _____	1am _____
4pm _____	2am + _____

1. What do you like or enjoy the most about your routine?

2. What about your routine is not so good or causes you difficulty?

3. How are your health, finances, relationships, and achievements?

4. How could things be better? What would have to change?

What are the costs & benefits of maintaining my current behavior?

Cost of staying the same	Benefit of staying the same
Health -	Health -
Relationships-	Relationships -
Finances -	Finances -
Career/work -	Career/work -
Legal -	Legal -

What are the costs & benefits of changing?

Cost of Changing	Benefit of Changing
Health -	Health -
Relationships-	Relationships -
Finances -	Finances -
Career/work -	Career/work -
Legal -	Legal -

WHAT IS IMPORTANT TO ME:

Everyone has things they believe in, standards to live by, or values. However, sometimes we act in ways that do not protect the things we value most or match our values. We may be tired, distracted by other things, or forgetful. Take some time here to remember your values and record them.

1. What are some of your strong personal beliefs and values? For example, some people believe strongly in being honest, assisting others, or helping their families. What are some things that you believe make a person a "good" person, son/daughter, mother/father, friend, or student? If you could be the best "you" you could be what qualities would you have.
Make a list here of values/traits or actions that you believe are most meaningful and important, then circle the two you feel are most essential to you right now. You may want to number them so that you put them in order of importance.

2. Is there anything that is getting in the way of your living by these standards? What may stand in the way of your being the best you can be? What would have to change for you to live more closely by your most important values and beliefs?

FUTURE INTENTION

"Night & Day dream of what you intend to do, and what you intend to be, and those dreams will interpret your intentions, let no doubt enter your intentions" - Dr. Wayne Dyer
Hold an Image of the life you want in mind and that image will become reality.

Often it is helpful to take the time to look ahead in our lives. Having an intention or a mental picture of how we would like things to be in the future can help us to feel less anxious, help us to maintain direction/focus, and help us to plan our time to move closer to our hopes and dreams. We **always** move in the direction of our most dominant thinking.

1. What are your **hopes, intentions, and dreams for the future**? Be specific. Fill in the details. Imagine you can have anything you want for yourself. What would that be?

2. What are things you can do **less of** to make these intentions a reality? What other things would you like to become involved in that would be helpful to replace the time spent on less helpful actions/behaviors?

3. What are you doing and can you do **more of beginning now** in your life to help you make these intentions reality? What new things would you like to become involved in?

I AM SUCCESSFUL

Sometimes we get disheartened when we forget the times that we have been successful at making changes in our lives or achieving something we wanted very much. **Everyone has been successful** at making changes in their life at some point or time. If you are alive, you had a successful birth. Let's use this exercise to remember your personal successes.

1. List some positive changes you have made in your life.

2. **Pick one** of the changes you listed above, maybe the one that was hardest to accomplish or that you feel most proud of, and list the following:

a. When did you start thinking about making the change? What was happening in your life at the time?

b. Did you make the change all at once or take small steps?

c. What did you do all at once or what were the steps?

d. How do you feel about the change today?

<u>STRENGTHS</u>

Sometimes we forget how powerful we can be if we need to. Let's look at the ways in which we are personally strong and powerful.

1. List your personal strengths and strong points:

2. How can these traits assist you in making changes in your life?

3. What could hinder your progress towards change?

4. How will your strengths help remove obstacles to your future?

<u>CHANGE PLAN & INTENTION WORKSHEET</u>:

The changes I want to make (or continue making) are: I intend to
The most important reason(s) for wanting these changes to happen are:
The specific steps I plan to take in changing are:
The specific ways other people can help and support me are:
I will know my intention is working if these favorable outcomes manifest in my life:
Some specific obstacles, things that could slow me down, or things that could get in my way are:
What I will do if my plan needs to be adjusted or is not completely effective:

CHANGE PLAN WORKSHEET (explanation/ examples)

The changes I want to make (or continue making) are: I intend to
List specific areas or ways in which you want to change. List specific goals or targets. Include positive goals for starting & creating change, increasing, and final improvements or modifications (fine tuning) of behavior.

The most important reason(s) for wanting these changes to happen are:
What are the most likely results of changing vs. staying the same?
What reasons for changing are the most significant for you and those close to you? What will be the emotional results of changing?

The specific steps I plan to take in changing are:
What are the steps in your plan to achieve your goals? What are some of the first steps included in this plan that you might accomplish most quickly? Be specific on how, when, and where, you will make these steps happen.

The specific ways other people can help and support me are:
Who will you seek out to assist & support your intentions? List specific ways that others (friends, family, counselors, etc.) can help to support you in your endeavor to change. How will you get others to help out?

I will know my intention is working if these favorable outcomes manifest in my life: *What do you expect will happen as a consequence of the change? What advantages will you obtain from the change? What will show you that you are successful?*

Some specific obstacles, things that could slow me down, or things that could get in my way are: *Anticipate any situations or difficulties you might possibly need to confront. What could possibly go wrong? What will help you stick to the plan regardless of problems or delays? How will you navigate obstacles and reach your destination?*

What I will do if my plan needs to be adjusted or is not completely effective: *List steps towards problem solution or some reorganizing strategies that you would use. Who would you approach for advice, support, or help? Where else might you turn for answers?*

The focus of this program is to assist people in making a change in their lives. Often, that change is to quit a habit, eliminate behaviors, or increase constructive, helpful activities. However, whatever the focus of transformation for you, any improvement in life you are considering is important. Please write in the space provided below what primary change, if any, you are considering now in your life.

Goal for Change: _____

On the following 0 - 5 scale, please rate the significance **to you** of making this transformation in your life (or continuing one already begun). Please circle the number that most closely matches **the importance of this change to your life**.

0	1	2	3	4	5
Not Significant					*Most*
AT ALL					*Significant*
					Thing in Life

Sometimes, even when goals/changes are important to us, we are still not sure that we can be successful in accomplishing them. Please circle the number that most closely matches **the confidence you have that you can successfully make the transformation you desire**.

0	1	2	3	4	5
Not Sure					*Completely*
At All					*Sure*

Sometimes, even though we know a change is important to us and we are certain we can make it happen, we aren't really looking forward to making a change (or continuing one already begun). Please circle the number that most closely matches **how much you really desire to make this change happen NOW.**

0	1	2	3	4	5
Fear Making					*Energized About*
The Change					*Making the*
					Change

Examine Your Answers

If you have less than a "5" rating on the Importance scale and it is not a zero, then why is the rating not lower? Why is it not a zero or a number lower than what you have chosen? Please explain as best you can.

If you have less than a "5" rating on the Importance scale or a zero, how could it become more important to you? Then, what would have to happen to move your rating up just one more? What would make it become a "5"?

If you have less than a "5" rating on the Confidence scale and it is not a zero, then why is the rating not lower? Why is it not a zero or a number lower than what you have chosen? Please explain as best you can.

If you have less than a "5" rating on the Confidence scale or a zero, how could it become more important to you? Then, what would have to happen to move your rating up just one more? What would make it become a "5"?

If you have less than a "5" rating on the Desire scale and it is not a zero, then why is the rating not lower? Why is it not a zero or a number lower than what you have chosen? Please explain as best you can.

If you have less than a "5" rating on the Desire scale or a zero, how could it become more important to you? Then, what would have to happen to move your rating up just one more? What would make it become a "5"?

Michael S. McGee

LPC, DCH, MS

Michael McGee has a Doctorate in Clinical Hypnotherapy, a Master's Degree in Counseling Psychology and is a Licensed Professional Counselor with a private practice in Southwest Virginia. He also works in acute care of mental health issues with clients in a community setting where he specifically treats those who suffer from anxiety, depression, PTSD, psychosis, suicide ideation, and homicide ideation in effort to prevent the need for inpatient hospitalization and reduce the need for psychiatric medication.

He is a member of the American Society of Clinical Hypnosis. He is a past member of the International Medical & Dental Hypnotherapy Association and the National Association of Transpersonal Hypnotherapy with specialized training for weight loss hypnosis, smoking cessation hypnosis, hypnoanesthesia, PTSD, and hypnotic regression.

He is an accomplished presenter and has contributed programs for the American Society of Clinical Hypnosis, National Association of Transpersonal Hypnotherapy, and Creative Alternatives in Therapy Conferences sponsored by Radford University for the past ten years. These include presentations such as, Addictions Hypnosis, PTSD treatment, Motivational Interviewing, Cognitive Hypnotherapy, Integrating Spirituality into Counseling, Modern Culture and Relapse Prevention, and Adolescents & Archetypes – Transpersonal Therapeutic Approaches.

He has taught various courses in Psychology at a small liberal arts university where he educated multiple sections combined of Abnormal Psychology, Adolescent Psychology, Child -Developmental Psychology, Introduction to Psychology, Personality, and Social Psychology.